I0100096

CRIME &

INCOMPETENCE

Guide to America's Immigration Crisis

ONE ROCK INK PUBLISHING

MARINKA PESCHMANN

Crime & Incompetence: Guide to America's Immigration Crisis

Copyright © 2013 Marinka Peschmann

All rights reserved. No part of this book may be reproduced in any form or by any means, electronic or mechanical, photocopying, scanning, or otherwise, including information storage and retrieval systems, without permission in writing from the publisher, except by a reviewer who may quote brief passages in a review.

First Edition
ISBN: 978-0-9878343-4-8
Library of Congress information available.

Published by One Rock Ink Publishing
Canada

Printed in the United States

DEDICATION

To the people who stand firm against crime and corruption.

MARINKA PESCHMANN

Contents

INTRODUCTION

Immigrant voters played a pivotal role in President Barack Obama's 2012 re-election win with Latinos making up 10 percent of the electorate, and voting for President Obama over Mitt Romney 71 percent to 27 percent. As a result, comprehensive immigration reform was anticipated to be back in the news and on Washington's agenda.[1] And so it is. It is President Obama's "top legislative priority for 2013."[2]

Once again Americans have been hearing lofty rhetoric from politicians on both sides of the aisle declaring that America's immigration system is "broken," and how they support "legal" immigration and reform.

Recently, senior Obama administration officials told the *New York Times,* "President Obama plans to push Congress to move quickly … on an ambitious overhaul of the immigration system that would include a path to citizenship for most of the 11 million illegal immigrants in the country."[3]

But what Americans are never told is what "legal" immigration has looked like for the legal immigrants who have sought the American dream; who have followed the law in a "broken" immigration system—a state-run bureaucracy affecting America's economy, national security, *and elections*. No one addresses how the broken immigration system has in large part contributed to the illegal alien/undocumented worker crisis in the first place.

And if Washington maintains its current modus operandi, it will stay that way.

As Senator Marco Rubio (R-FL) recently explained, "Policies matter. And look, the Republican Party does have a challenge. We can't just be the anti-illegal immigration party. We have to be the pro-legal immigration party." Senator Rubio has been calling to pass a series of bills which would include a version of the DREAM Act whereby children who were brought to the U.S. unlawfully would receive some type of legal status.

Since then, some Republican senators have sponsored the Achieve Act, a watered-down version of the Democrats' DREAM Act.[4] The shift continues within the Republican Party, with senators like John McCain (R-AZ) now throwing his full support behind the Democrats' DREAM Act and a path to citizenship for illegal aliens/undocumented workers.[5]

Only in Washington can the word "children" be radically redefined; and no one in the media calls out the politicians. Babies are children; so are infants, toddlers, four-year-olds, six-year-olds, and ten-year-olds up to puberty. But babies and toddlers who were brought to the U.S. illegally can't vote for eighteen years. One-year-olds can't vote for seventeen years, and so forth, which is why these "children" do not benefit from the DREAM Act.

In Washington, the definition of "children" has been redefined to include those "children" from sixteen to thirty-five years old.[6] Is it a coincidence that this Washingtonian re-definition of "children" includes "children" who were brought to the US illegally who can now vote or will soon be able to vote?

What about the babies and toddlers who will one day grow up and want to work legally in America? Who is advocating for them? No one.

This book is not a one-sided political attack, however, because *both* political parties are responsible for America's immigration crisis. *Crime & Incompetence: Guide to America's Immigration Crisis* is not about left or right, but right and wrong.

This book will give you the information you need to actually fix the immigration crisis by exposing why it is so broken.

So, take off your ideological glasses here. It is time for a serious reality check.

First, let's cut to the chase. Both Republican and Democrat administrations have refused to secure America's borders despite promising to do so to get elected. Unsecured borders are an obvious contributing factor to the immigration crisis. The very fact that both political parties (under Bush, Clinton, Bush, and now Obama) have all refused to secure America's borders should tell you all that you need to know about how insincere America's elected leaders have been about fixing the "problem."

7

But the borders are only one piece of the problem. The other piece is how the Washington establishment is largely responsible for America's broken "legal" immigration system, another factor that has contributed to the number of illegal aliens in America.

After reading *Crime & Incompetence: Guide to America's Immigration Crisis*, Americans will learn the dirty little secret Washington politicos do not want them to know: how under both Republican (Bush & Bush) and Democratic (Clinton & Obama) administrations' watches, the United States Citizenship and Immigration Services (USCIS), formerly the Immigration and Nationalization Services (INS), grew into a dysfunctional bureaucracy that is riddled with crime, corruption, and incompetence.

Worse, the USCIS is an agency that is arguably an *anti-legal immigration* agency that still faces challenges processing legal immigrants (despite receiving almost $1 billion to modernize), yet somehow, magically, is expected to efficiently process President Obama's executive order immigration policies—and potentially a "bi-partisan" path to citizenship, a.k.a. amnesty for millions of illegal aliens.

Newsflash: according to a recent Government Accountability Office (GAO) report, the USCIS has already spent about $703 million as part of their so-called transformation and modernization program for legal immigration—that's about "$292 million more than the original" estimate and the dollar amount is still climbing. As the GAO report warns: the USCIS does not operate using "best practices." Therefore, it makes "meaningful measurement and oversight of program status and progress, and accountability for results, difficult to achieve."[7]

This is the government agency that would be tasked to process millions of illegals?!

How can an agency that cannot process legal immigrants competently be expected to process millions of illegal/undocumented workers properly?

What about granting citizenship to the legal immigrants stuck in backlogs and bureaucracy for years or decades? There are also legal immigrants (those on work visas trying to adjust their status to permanent resident/Green card) who have been paying U.S. taxes for years, including into Social Security that they may never see (if the broken bureaucracy kicks them out or the wait times wear them down). What about them? Who is fighting for the legal immigrants?

Ask the politicians who support comprehensive immigration reform to find out. That would include most Democrats from President Obama, Vice President Joe Biden, Senate Majority Leader Harry Reid (D-NV), Chuck Schumer (D-NY), Dick Durbin (D-IL), Bob Menendez (D-NJ), and Michael Bennet (D-CO), to Republican senators including John McCain (R-AZ), Lindsey Graham, (R-SC), Jeff Flake (R-AZ), and Marco Rubio (R-FL), part of the so-called "Gang of Eight."[8]

Here's another newsflash: throwing money at the USCIS is not going to fix the problem.

After reading this book you will see that the immigration system is not broken because of a lack of funds. The problem is always the same, and it has been for decades: the agency's chronic mismanagement; leadership defects; arcane, arbitrary bureaucracy; and flawed, outdated immigration policies and quotas.

Okay. I promise. This is the last you will hear about politics.

In *Crime & Incompetence: Guide to America's Immigration Crisis—* Americans will also get a taste for what life is like for legal immigrants living at the mercy of faceless bureaucrats, in a broken agency that controls their destiny, freedom, and ability to provide for themselves and their families while stuck in backlogs facing mind-bending incompetence. While many Americans take their freedoms for granted, legal immigrants stuck in a broken system do not take their freedom for granted because they are never truly free.

This book is a stark departure from my other books.

Instead of a narrative-fact-driven book, this book is a cover-to-cover collection of open sources, sometimes from media outlets, other times from non-partisan government reports, criminal indictments, and selections from my prior reporting that shows the history of legal immigration since 1986 when President Ronald Reagan last passed amnesty (promising it would fix the system then) to the present. In every instance, with each bullet point and summary, there is an endnote with online links for you to go to the original sources to find out more about the problem or incident.

This book contains my research from years of covering the INS/USCIS agency.

It is a handbook of unvarnished information and resources that I encourage you to read near a computer (if you are reading this in paperback version) so you can easily access the original sources to find out more.

Once you reach Chapter 3, where the Broken Immigration Timeline portion of the book begins, aside from *Alerts!* (e.g., *Crime Alerts! Sex Alerts! National Security Alert!*) there will be little editorial on my part, because the facts speak for themselves.

Only by seeing the facts will Americans finally get a clear picture of the immigration crisis.

Now, welcome to legal immigration and to the world of crime, corruption, and incompetence at America's immigration agency.

—Marinka Peschmann

1·

LEGAL IN AMERICA? NOT SO FAST

First, let's talk truth about legal immigration.

Legal immigration can be like going to Vegas. Some people fly through the system or win a Green card in the "diversity visa program" lottery while others get stuck in backlogs and bureaucracy for years if not decades.[9]

There are two ways to legally obtain permanent residency in America and a Green card. Either the immigrant is sponsored by an employer (employment-based) or a family member (family-based). Under these two main categories, several other sub-categories emerge. To keep it simple, take a look at the charts below. It shows what "waiting-in-line" and "backlogs" mean for legal immigrants from different countries.

Below are simplified versions of the State Department Visa Bulletin for legal immigrants who filed under the EB (employment-based) category that I have recreated from Trackitt.com reflecting two different months, July and December 2012. The monthly Visa Bulletins provide the "priority dates" (as the government bureaucrats hilariously, seriously call them) for legal immigrants who have approved "labor certifications."

Obtaining a "labor certification" in itself is a lengthy, challenging process, but for the sake of brevity: the employer/sponsor must prove that the legal immigrant is NOT taking a job away from an American, and that they can pay the immigrant the "prevailing wage" according to the Labor Department.[10] It is worth noting that powerful unions work closely with the Labor Department including the American Federation of Government Employees (AFGE), Service Employees International Union (SEIU), and the American Federation of Labor and Congress of Industrial Organizations (AFL-CIO).[11] All applications start at the USCIS, but it is the Department of Labor that approves and certifies a labor certification that the legal immigrant needs *before moving* onto *this line* (in the chart below) for the "priority date" step with the State Department.

Category Employment Based	Cutoff Date (July 2012 Visa Bulletin)	Cutoff Date (Previous Bulletin)
EB2 China	15 August 2007	15 August 2007
EB2 India	15 August 2007	15 August 2007
EB3 China	22 September 2005 ▲	08 August 2005
EB3 India	22 September 2002 ▲	15 September 2002
EB3 Mexico	22 July 2006 ▲	08 June 2006
EB3 Philippines	08 June 2006 ▲	22 May 2006
EB3 ROW	22 July 2006 ▲	08 June 2006

[**Source:** State Department][12].

These two first charts show legal immigrants who filed under the EB-2 and EB-3 categories (there is EB-1, 2, 3, 4, 5 ... etc.). The EB numbers reflect different skill sets, including unskilled workers. EB-3 is the professional category for instance, although there are different "professional" categories. To see all the different categories, go to link provided at the USCIS website.[13] If I listed them all here, your head would explode.

Now compare the State Department Visa Bulletin for July (above) with the Bulletin for December 2012.

Category Employment-Based	Cutoff Date (December 2012 Visa Bulletin)	Cutoff Date (Previous Bulletin)
EB2 China	22 October 2007	01 September 2007
EB2 India	01 September 2004	01 September 2004
EB3 China	01 July 2006 ▲	15 April 2006
EB3 India	01 November 2002 ▲	22 October 2002
EB3 Mexico	22 December 2006 ▲	22 November 2006
EB3 Philippines	15 August 2006 ▲	08 August 2006
EB3 ROW	22 December 2006 ▲	22 November 2006

[**Source:** State Department][14]

No, your eyes are not deceiving you and there are no typos. If you go back to prior Visa Bulletins, you will see how sometimes the "priority" dates move ahead (hence the arrows in the chart), stay the same, or they go *backwards*. That's legal immigration; where your guess is as good as mine. The best a legal immigrant can do is to hope for the best, expect the worst, follow the trends, and pray they do not get knocked out of line when arbitrary rules change or the USCIS loses their file along the way (more on this in the timeline section).

Let's break the charts down further.

Legal immigrants with *approved labor certifications* by the above "priority" dates may now move onto the next step, the I-485: the "Application to Register Permanent Residence or Adjust Status" (FBI background check which includes fingerprinting) and the I-693: the "Report of Medical Examination and Vaccination Record," and wait in this line.

But living in limbo and waiting for years is just part of the fun. The USCIS has come up with ways to make it even more impossible for legal immigrants to be processed (in part to clear out their chronic backlogs) and *kick them* out of line.

Here's how they do it. While legal immigrants wait in line, the USCIS can send out what are called RFE's (request for more evidence) to their sponsors. Why? Because things change while legal immigrants have been waiting in line for over ten years (see India) or over six years (see Mexico, Philippines, or ROW countries like Canada, etc.), which could mean the legal immigrant is then denied. Realities include such things as whether or not the company that sponsored the immigrant still exists. Does the job still exist? If the answer is yes, can the company still afford to pay the prevailing wage according to the Labor Department? Is the petitioner/immigrant still alive? But it gets worse; the wait times for legal immigrants who petitioned under family-based applications are even *longer* than those who filed under employment-based applications.

State Department Visa Bulletin for December 2012.[15]

Family Sponsored	All Chargeability Areas Except Those Listed	CHINA – Mainland born	INDIA
F1	01 Dec. 2005	01 Dec. 2005	01 Dec. 2005
F2A	22 Aug. 2010	22 Aug. 2010	22 Aug. 2010
F2B	15 Nov. 2004	15 Nov. 2004	15 Nov. 2004
F3	08 June 2002	08 June 2002	08 June 2002
F4	01 April 2001	01 April 2001	01 April 2001
Family Sponsored	MEXICO	PHILIP-PINES	
FI	01 July 1993	08 Oct. 1997	
F2A	01 Aug. 2010	22 Aug. 2010	
F2B	15 Nov. 1992	22 Mar. 2002	
F3	01 Mar. 1993	01 Aug. 1992	
F4	22 July 1996	22 Mar. 1989	

The chart above shows legal immigrants who filed under the "limited" Family Preference Visa, (FB-1, FB-2, FB-3, etc.) as opposed to the "unlimited" immediate relative (IR) immigrant visa category (IR-1, IR-2 etc.). The IR visa types are based on a close family relationship with a U.S. citizen such as a spouse.

The FB category breaks down like this:

Family Preference Immigrant Visas (Limited): These visa types are for specific, more distant, family relationships with a U.S. citizen and some specified relationships with a Lawful Permanent Resident (LPR). There are fiscal year numerical limitations on family preference immigrants, shown at the end of each category (the quotas). The **family preference categories** are:

- **Family First Preference (F1):** Unmarried sons and daughters of U.S. citizens, and their minor children, if any. (23,400)
- **Family Second Preference (F2):** Spouses, minor children, and unmarried sons and daughters (age 21 and over) of LPRs.

At least 77 percent of all visas available for this category will go to the spouses and children; the remainder is allocated to unmarried sons and daughters. (114,200)

- **Family Third Preference (F3):** Married sons and daughters of U.S. citizens, and their spouses and minor children. (23,400)
- **Family Fourth Preference (F4):** Brothers and sisters of U.S. citizens, and their spouses and minor children, provided the U.S. citizens are at least 21 years of age. (65,000)[16]

So to break it down, if you are from the Philippines and you filed under the family-based category F4 and you were approved in March of 1989, your number has come up after *twenty-four years* of waiting. People from Mexico who filed under the F2B category who were approved in November 1992 after a twenty-one-year wait get to move to the next step and so forth.

But these legal immigrants who played by the rules cannot get too excited yet that they will obtain a Green card because they are not finished either. Like the employment-based legal immigrants, the family-based immigrants also have to complete the 1-485 (the FBI background check step), and 1-693 (the medical step), before they are finished and able to live and work freely in America.

As you can see, the immigration debate in Washington is upside down. How many times have we heard from politicians, pro-amnesty groups, and some churches speaking passionately about the humanity and compassion for illegal aliens—yet they remain silent about the humanity and compassion for legal immigrants? If anyone should be put on a path to citizenship, shouldn't it be the legal immigrants who followed the law in a broken system as opposed to lawbreakers? Let's be blunt here. Legal immigrants following the rules can die waiting in line before they are processed from start to finish. Now are you starting to see why there is an illegal immigration problem in America?

While politicians sometimes acknowledge that there are long wait times for legal immigrants and insist the illegal aliens/undocumented workers will go to the end of the line, they seem incapable (for good reason) of spelling out what "waiting in line" and going to "the end of the line" really means. Perhaps that is because if Americans knew that the end of the line begins over two decades from now (thus exposing the politicians' ridiculous promises), they would be laughed out of office. Is Washington seriously going to start a path to citizenship/amnesty over *twenty-four years* from now? It wouldn't be "fair" if the illegal aliens/undocumented workers got to cut into a shorter legal immigrant wait line, right?

That's not going to happen. You are being lied to. If President Obama and Washington politicians pass any type of status to illegal aliens/undocumented workers before legalizing legal immigrants who have played by the rules (and those who were worn down or incorrectly denied because of the travesty of legal immigration), it is nothing more than a slap in the face to legal immigrants, including those from Mexico, India, China, Philippines, Canada, Europe, Australia, Haiti, Thailand, Russia, Singapore, UK, Africa, Middle East, South America, and all around the world.[17] What would you do if you were a legal immigrant stuck in this system—withdraw your application and go illegal because following the law in America is for suckers? It is also a slap in the face to Americans who expect a competent government that upholds the rule of law and serves the people instead of themselves.

Only in Washington can politicians like the Gang of Eight: Chuck Schumer (D-NY), Dick Durbin (D-IL), Bob Menendez (D-NJ), and Michael Bennet (D-CO), John McCain (R-AZ), Lindsey Graham, (R-SC), Jeff Flake (R-AZ), and Marco Rubio (R-FL) discriminate against *all* legal immigrants from every country in the world and be self-congratulatory about it.[18] Who is going to play the race card now? The self-righteous hypocrisy is mind-numbing. Now that you know the truth about the wait times, you can call Washington out on their empty words and absurd promises.

FUN FACT FOR LEGAL IMMIGRANTS (bureaucracy at work)

Following is how legal immigration receipt numbers are explained (LIN, SRC, EAC, WAC).

The receipt number is one of the most commonly used numbers, by immigrants and lawyers alike, to track the progress or identify a particular immigration case or filing.

These receipt numbers start with three letters, followed by a series of numbers, for example EAC-06-123-45678. Here is how to understand what the numbers mean.

The first three letters indicate the USCIS service center which is processing the petition, as follows:
- EAC - Vermont Service Center;
- WAC - California Service Center;
- LIN - Nebraska Service Center; and
- SRC - Texas Service Center.

The next two digits represent the fiscal year in which USCIS received the petition. In the example above, "06" means that the petition was received by USCIS during Fiscal Year 2006. The next three digits represent the computer workday on which the receipt was processed and the fee was taken. Finally, the last five digits are used to uniquely identify the petition filed.[19] Welcome to a taste of life at the hands of a state-run bureaucracy. Imagine—this could be your future, steering through ObamaCare rules and regulations. You are not a person, just a bunch of numbers.

HANDY RESOURCE ALERT!

Trackitt.com is an excellent resource for learning about legal immigration. It is like a help board for legal immigrants to assist one another in navigating through the confusing, nonsensical, and evolving legal immigration process. You can follow their stories and see the challenges and successes. Take a look at the home page and imagine the petition category numbers being replaced for healthcare (hip replacement, breast cancer, etc.). Living at the mercy of faceless bureaucrats can be scary stuff.

2 ·

TAKE A WALK IN THE SHOES OF
LEGAL IMMIGRANTS

What people may not realize or have considered is that most legal immigrants are unwilling to speak out about the problems and crime at America's immigration agency because they are living at the mercy of government bureaucrats *at the agency*.

Government bureaucrats who hold their future, their freedom, their lives, their livelihood in their hands while immigrants anxiously wait to be processed, approved or *denied*. Nobody has the right to live in America. It is a privilege just like nobody has the right to live in any country. But when legal immigrants apply and their applications are accepted by the USCIS (and their checks are cashed) it is with the reasonable expectation that they will be processed and receive a "yes" or "no" decision as to whether or not they can legally come or stay in America or must leave. As you will see in the broken immigration timeline section that's not what necessarily happens for years, decades, if ever.

This is also why combating crime and corruption at the agency is difficult. Imagine if you were dealing with an immigration consultant, paid a fee and they took off with your money. What would you do?

Imagine if a federal immigration official asked you for a bribe (they call them tips, not bribes), what would you do? Most Americans would probably call the police but for legal immigrants stuck in the broken immigration system calling the police may not be an option, simply because the repercussion including the possibility of deportation would silence them.

Indeed, government workers wield that kind of life-changing power over legal immigrants—daily. It is a constant worry that hovers over legal immigrants facing such an uncertain future for such a long time.

Words cannot adequately describe how a legal immigrant's heart races every time they receive an envelope from the USCIS. Is it good news, another hoop to jump through, or the dreaded denial? A faceless bureaucrat can stamp an application with a denial and in an instant a legal immigrant's entire life has been ripped out from under them. This is especially earth shattering for the legal immigrants who worked legally in the U.S. on work visas for years, paid taxes, bought homes, built lives, and applied for permanent residency in the meantime—only to be denied years later and literally kicked out of the country.

Now the legal immigrant is not legal anymore and they have been told by America's immigration agency that they have thirty, sixty or so days to leave the country or be deported and barred from entering the U.S. for five or ten years. As I previously mentioned, Americans take their freedoms for granted, but not legal immigrants who suffer in silence because of what the politicians effortlessly call "broken immigration."

Ironic, it is so easy for America's immigration agency to kick out legal immigrants but not illegal aliens. That is probably because legal immigrants provide their contact information when they file their applications seeking legal status. This is the upside down world legal immigrants have to deal with.[20] So first, please read some the stories of legal immigrants that appeared in the *New York Times*. It will give you some more context to the crime, corruption and incompetence that follows in the upcoming broken immigration timeline chapters.

Following is an excerpt:

"In early March Mr. Harris's wife, Claudia Solano-Lopez, and their three small children left their home in Raleigh, N.C., to move to Mexico City. To comply with immigration law, the family now must live apart for two years.

Mr. Harris, who is 37 and a veteran of the first Persian Gulf war, met his future wife in 1997 when they both were studying for doctoral degrees in food science at Ohio State University. They married in 2001. They completed their Ph.D.s, and last year Mr. Harris became an assistant professor at North Carolina State University.

Ms. Solano-Lopez, 45, had come from Mexico on a visa for advanced studies (its official name is J-1) that requires immigrants to return to their home countries for at least two years after completing their academic work. Distressed by the prospect of separation and its impact on their children (3-year-old twins and a toddler), Mr. Harris and his wife consulted several lawyers. On their advice, they applied for a hardship waiver from the two-year foreign residency rule, as it is known.

"We understood that we were doing the correct thing, and this waiver was the way we would keep our family together," Mr. Harris said. But the letter they received from Citizenship and Immigration Services denying the waiver said the family's separation would not be "exceptional hardship."

"If they think this is minor emotional anguish, they don't know what they are talking about," Mr. Harris said.

With his first-year professor's schedule and salary, he felt he could not care for their three children alone in Raleigh. The couple did not appeal the waiver denial, because their lawyers said their chances of success were small.

Noting that many Mexicans live illegally in North Carolina, Mr. Harris said, "I feel this is almost a punishment for following the rules.""

To read more legal immigrant stories visit *New York Times* link:[21]

PONZI SCHEME ALERT!

Because America's immigration agency is partially funded by user fees (what legal immigrants pay to have their applications processed), the agency never declines any new applications even though they know these new legal immigrants cannot be processed from start to finish for years, decades—if ever. Reminiscent to how Social Security is structured where new workers fund the benefits paid out to retirees, America's immigration agency depends on new legal immigrants to remain operational. As you will see in the broken immigration timeline chapters, U.S. taxpayers are not off the hook.

BROKEN IMMIGRATION TIMELINE

MARINKA PESCHMANN

3 •

PRESIDENT RONALD REAGAN ERA

Reagan era: 1986

MARRIAGE FRAUD ALERT!

As you will see later on marriage fraud remains a problem today.

• Source: Government and Accountability Office Report (GAO):
Marriage Fraud: Controls in Most Countries Surveyed Stronger Than
in U.S. Jul 14, 1986, summary below:[22]

Pursuant to a congressional request, GAO surveyed 12 other
countries to determine what controls they use to prevent immigration
marriage fraud. Congress is considering legislation to curb such fraud,
which involves aliens and citizens or permanent residents entering
marriages of convenience to change the aliens' immigration status.
    GAO found that: (1) the Immigration and Naturalization Service
(INS) estimated that nearly *30 percent* of the alien spouses who
entered the United States in 1984 were involved in suspicious marital
relationships; and (2) from 1978 to 1985, the total number of
immigrants dropped 5.2 percent, but the number of immigrants
acquiring status as spouses increased 59 *percent. GAO also found that
other countries use a variety of measures to curb immigration marriage fraud,
including: (1) requiring alien spouses to fulfill conditional residency requirements
and furnish evidence of a continuing marital relationship; (2) requiring alien
fiancees to have personally met their future spouses before visa approval; (3)
imposing criminal penalties or deportation for aliens who attempt to procure
immigrant status by marriage fraud; and (4) notifying immigration officials when
a marriage involving an alien is terminated.* GAO noted that Congress is
considering legislation that would include such measures [italics
mine].

AMNESTY ALERT!

Under President Ronald Reagan Americans were told that America's immigration problems would be solved because of the Immigration Reform and Control Act of 1986 which granted amnesty to millions of illegal aliens ... did not quite work out that way.

• Excerpt of President Ronald Reagan's Remarks on Signing the Immigration Reform and Control Act of 1986. November 6, 1986.[23]

The President: I'm very pleased that you could all be here today. This bill, the Immigration Reform and Control Act of 1986, that I will sign in a few minutes is the most comprehensive reform of our immigration laws since 1952. It's the product of one of the longest and most difficult legislative undertakings in the last three Congresses. Further, it's an excellent example of a truly successful bipartisan effort. The administration and the allies of immigration reform on both sides of the Capitol and both sides of the aisle worked together to accomplish these critically important reforms to control illegal immigration.

In 1981 this administration asked the Congress to pass a comprehensive legislative package, including employer sanctions, other measures to increase enforcement of the immigration laws, and legalization. The act provides these three essential components. Distance has not discouraged illegal immigration to the United States from all around the globe. The problem of illegal immigration should not, therefore, be seen as a problem between the United States and its neighbors. Our objective is only to establish a reasonable, fair, orderly, and secure system of immigration into this country and not to discriminate in any way against particular nations or people.

I would like to recognize a few of the public servants whose unflagging efforts have made this legislation a reality ... Important roles were played by Senator Strom Thurmond, Senator Paul Simon, and Congressmen Ham Fish, Bill McCollum, Chuck Schumer, and many others in both Houses of the Congress and in both parties. Additionally, I would like to note the excellent efforts of members of my administration who have worked so hard over the last 6 years to make this bill signing possible today.

Future generations of Americans will be thankful for our efforts to humanely regain control of our borders and thereby preserve the value of one of the most sacred possessions of our people: American citizenship. So, now I'll get on with the signing and make this into law. Hope nothing happens to me between here and the table. [Laughter]

AMNESTY FAILS ALERT!

Less than one year later, instead of solving America's immigration crisis, amnesty expands.

• **U.S. is expanding amnesty program for illegal aliens—** headline, *New York Times*, April 6, 1987. "New rules drafted by the Agriculture Department define "perishable commodities" far more broadly than expected by sponsors of the legislation. As a result, more aliens will qualify, and intense debate over the wisdom of the new rules is likely in Congress …The special amnesty program for farm workers was indispensable to passage of the immigration bill. Representative Charles E. Schumer of Brooklyn, one of three Democrats who devised the program said it was not meant for producers of tobacco or hops. The broad definition of perishable commodities, like the special program for farm workers, reflects the economic and political importance of farmers, who have lobbied the Agriculture Department in the five months since Mr. Reagan signed the Immigration Reform and Control Act of 1986."[24]

INCOMPETENCE ALERT!

Two years later Congress is unable to track the success or failure of President Reagan's so-called one-time amnesty solution.

• **Source: Government and Accountability Office Report:** Studies of the Immigration Control Act's Impact on Mexico Feb 17, 1988, summary below.[25]

In response to a congressional request, GAO: (1) reviewed information and research studies pertaining to emigration from

Mexico to the United States; and (2) summarized information relevant to an assessment of the impact on Mexico of the Immigration Reform and Control Act of 1986 (IRCA). GAO found that: (1) it was too early to determine the full impact of the act, since the enforcement of employer sanctions did not begin until June 1987; *(2) there was no evidence of mass deportation of undocumented Mexican nationals from the United States; and (3) there was no information on the Mexican returnee population and its impact on Mexico. GAO also found that U.S. and Mexican researchers agree that there will be problems in measuring the U.S. immigration reform's impact because of a lack of: (1) data consistency; (2) systematic data collection; (3) baseline data on the Mexican labor market prior to IRCA; and (4) coordination between data sources and researchers.* GAO noted that researchers and policy analysts urge a bilateral approach to resolving immigration issues resulting from IRCA [italics mine].

FAILED POLITICIAN ALERT!

Senator Charles "Chuck" Schumer (D-NY) was singled out by President Reagan as among the public servants who made his [amnesty] legislation a reality." It failed miserably and America's immigration problem has never been fixed since then. Fast-forward to today.

In January 2013 Senator Schumer with the 'Gang of Eight' senators introduced a "framework" to solve America's immigration crisis that includes another path to citizenship for roughly 11 million illegal immigrants.[26] Didn't he get the memo about the last one that failed to fix the immigration crisis?

FANTASY ALERT!

No one including politicians have any idea as to how many illegal aliens/undocumented workers are in America because there is no place for them to go to check-in. Illegal aliens probably would not check-in even if there were some place to go.

So whenever you hear politicians claim today that they are crafting policy to legalize 11 million illegal aliens/undocumented workers that's just a lowball fantasy number just like it was when

President Reagan passed amnesty for 3 million people and the numbers soared. It's impossible for anyone to know how many illegal aliens/undocumented workers are in America. Your guess is as a good as mine.

4·

PRESIDENT GEORGE H.W. BUSH ERA

<u>H.W. Bush era: 1991</u>

INCOMPETENCE ALERT!

Less than five years after President Reagan's Immigration Reform and Control Act of 1986/amnesty America's immigration problems continue.

• **Source: Government and Accountability Office Report:** Actions Being Taken, But Problems Remain, Jun 24, 1991, summary below.[27]

GAO discussed Department of Justice (DOJ) and Immigration and Naturalization Service (INS) *efforts to address leadership and management problems.* GAO noted that INS: (1) implemented models for the Border Patrol and the adjudication program to better allocate staff based on work load; (2) requested increased staffing for detention centers; (3) initiated a management information planning process to help ensure more coordinated system development; and (4) initiated programs to address strategic planning weaknesses using a total-quality-management framework. GAO also noted that: (1) INS reduced the autonomy of its regional offices to promote uniformity of program operations, make it easier to effectively allocate and balance resources to address changing work loads, and increase accountability of field managers to INS headquarters; (2) *INS did not confront the dual enforcement structure and the unclear division of enforcement responsibilities between the Border Patrol and the Investigations Division;* (3) INS appointed a new Executive Associate Commissioner for Management, initiated joint audits with the Customs Service to help ensure the collection of inspection fees, and enacted a debt management program to improve the collection of bonds and other receivables; and (4) modification of the DOJ Financial Management Information System for INS use *continues to be delayed* [italics mine]."

H.W. Bush era: 1992

CORRUPTION ALERT!

• **Phila. man charged with bribing INS agent to obtain work cards**—headline, *Philadelphia Inquirer,* July 1, 1992. "The head of a North Philadelphia travel agency was accused by a federal grand jury yesterday of paying $7,200 in bribes to an undercover immigration official to obtain employment cards for illegal aliens. Teresita Bono, 41 ... was indicted on nine counts of bribery of a public official, payments allegedly made between July 3, 1990, and Feb. 12, 1991, to the undercover official working at the U.S. Immigration and Naturalization Service office."[28]

5·

PRESIDENT BILL CLINTON ERA

Clinton era: 1993

INCOMPETENCE ALERT!

Serious incompetence plagues America's immigration agency—management and service delivery problems. President George H.W. Bush hands President William Jefferson Clinton a mess.

• **Source: Government and Accountability Office Report:** Making Needed Policy and Management Decisions on Immigration Issues, Mar 30, 1993, summary below.[29]

GAO discussed the impact of immigration policy and management decisions on the Immigration and Naturalization Service's (INS) operations. GAO noted that: (1) *Congress and the administration need to resolve immigration policy issues on who should be permitted entry, what should be done to prevent illegal entry, and what should be done to remove illegal aliens; (2) INS needs strong leadership and management reforms to balance its roles of enforcement and service, and overcome continuing management and service delivery problems; (3) the INS budget development process has been inadequate, with little accountability for funds or attention to agency priorities; and (4) INS needs to develop a strategic vision of its operations* [italics mine].

INCOMPETENCE ALERT!

Seven years after Americans were promised the immigration crisis would be fixed the federal government still has not fixed it.

• **Source: Government and Accountability Office Report:**
Problems in Controlling the Flow of Illegal Aliens, Jun 30, 1993, summary below.[30]

GAO discussed the Immigration and Naturalization Service's (INS) efforts to address immigration enforcement problems and the administration's 1993 plan to *combat illegal alien smuggling by crime syndicates*. GAO noted that: (1) INS believes that the deterrent value of increased alien detention and preflight inspection programs could strengthen its illegal alien immigration control efforts; (2) *although the administration's 1993 plan to combat alien smuggling by crime syndicates involves strengthening law enforcement efforts, combatting smuggling at its source, interdicting and redirecting smuggling ships in transit, and expediting exclusion procedures processing, the plan does not address alien detention and removal barriers; (3) immigration policy, international relations, international economic disparity, and the lack of resources, detention space and sufficient penalties inhibit INS from deporting, excluding, and preventing the arrival of illegal aliens; and (4) Congress and the administration need to resolve border control and deportation issues before INS can be expected to effectively control illegal alien immigration* [italics mine].

ILLEGAL ALIEN ALERT!

Prominent lawyers and judges hire illegal aliens. Oh, the hypocrisy. Happened under President George W. Bush with DHS Chief Michael Chertoff too.

• **Clinton nominates Reno at Justice**—headline, *Washington Post*, February 12, 1993. "In December, Clinton nominated corporate lawyer Zoe E. Baird, who was forced to withdraw because she had violated immigration and tax laws in hiring illegal immigrants. He was poised to name federal judge Kimba M. Wood before she withdrew last week after the disclosure that she had also employed an illegal immigrant to care for her child."[31]

• **Homeland chief Michael Chertoff had home cleaned by illegal immigrants**—headline, *New York Daily News*, December 12, 2006.[32] "Since 2005, Chertoff has employed Maryland-based Consistent Cleaning Services - and its staff of illegal immigrants - to clean his suburban Washington home. Chertoff didn't know that some of the company's workers, who passed security checks by the Secret Service, were undocumented."

Clinton era: 1994

CRIME ALERT!

• **In immigration labyrinth, corruption comes easily**—headline, *New York Times,* September 12, 1994. "The word quickly spread through immigrant communities. Come to the… offices of the INS (now USCIS). Bring cash. Buy the right to live or work in the U.S.… Smooth-talking middlemen took care of the details, bribing immigration service employees… Every year dozens of INS employees are arrested… an investigation… during the past decade… found that the agency has repeatedly failed to shore up security weaknesses, even when corruption arrests have exposed them over and over again."[33]
• **One broker's slide into bribery**—headline, *New York Times,* September 12, 1994. "Across the country, thousands of people like them provide immigration advice at rates far below those charged by lawyers. (An application for political asylum, for example, might cost $2,500 if done by a lawyer; Mr. Escobar charged $700.) Many brokers offer legitimate services. But they also are prominent in corruption cases, both as bribers and as vendors of fraudulent documents. They are unlicensed and do not face the kind of bar association oversight that lawyers do … In the bribery schemes that beset the Washington office of the INS, the brokers profited the most. While the employees were typically making $100 per work card, the middlemen were charging immigrants $500 to $700. When the investigations were over, Mr. Escobar, Mr. Vera and four other brokers stood convicted of bribing Federal employees."[34]

Clinton era: 1996

PLAYING POLITICS ALERT!

Did the Clinton White House use the INS for political gain? According to David Schippers, Chief Investigative Counsel for the Clinton Impeachment investigations, in his book, *Sell Out: The Inside Story of President Clinton's Impeachment* (Regnery Publishing, Inc. 2000), the answer is yes.[35] The Clinton White politicized the INS when they exploited a program called Citizenship USA (CUSA) to naturalize (become U.S. citizens) legal immigrants (Green Card holders) in time to get the Democrat vote out for the 1996 Presidential elections. President Clinton with Vice President Al Gore put pressure on the already troubled INS to swiftly naturalize legal immigrants by short-circuiting background checks (finger prints submissions I-485), in time for them to register to vote. As a result felons are now American citizens. Meanwhile, their efforts also compounded the backlogs for legal immigrants waiting lawfully to be processed.

David Schippers, a Democrat, wanted to add this as part of the impeachment articles in 1998 but there was no time. It was swept under the rug and no one was held accountable for misusing the INS for political gain, thwarting the rule of law, and jeopardizing America's security. As you will see later in this timeline, President Barack Obama, thanks to President George W. Bush, will use a renamed version of the CUSA program as well— as did Bush.

Clinton era: 1997

CRIME & CORRUPTION ALERT!

• **The counterfeit Rockefeller**—headline, *Vanity Fair*, January 2001. "Even [Det. George Mueller at the Los Angeles District] got confused sorting through it all. *Bribery of federal passport officials*. A diamond-smuggling scheme in Zaire. An alleged perfume fraud involving Michael Jackson's brother Jermaine ... Another half-million or so swindled from a French singer ... Not to mention a shooting at an intersection in West Hollywood involving Dodi Fayed's Hummer. Oh, and the dead body. And the hand grenades in the space heater."[36],[37]

Clinton era: 1998

CRIME, CORRUPTION & SEX ALERT!

• **7 INS employees and 26 others are charged with selling false immigration papers**—headline, *New York Times*, March 13, 1998. "Seven employees of the INS (now USCIS) and 26 others had been charged with selling fraudulent immigration papers for more than

$100,000 in bribes. The case…continues to raise questions about how well the agency is addressing its vulnerability to corruption. The scheme grew so brazen, prosecutors said, that some cash bribes were exchanged right inside the INS offices …in downtown Manhattan."[38]

• **INS trainee indicted on charges of bribery and civil rights violations**—headline, *Siskind Susser Bland Newsletter,* September 12, 1998. "An Immigration and Naturalization Service inspector trainee at the Juarez-Lincoln Bridge at the U.S.-Mexican border has been indicted on charges of bribery and civil rights violations. The employee is 32-year-old Juan H. Villarreal and his indictment alleges that he accepted $400 on two occasions last year for illegally providing immigration documents to people crossing in to the U.S. from Mexico. Villarreal is also charged with transferring a fraudulent birth registration card.

Villarreal is also alleged to have demanded sex from a Mexican female in exchange for returning her immigration documents that had been seized and for allowing her to make illegal entry into the United States."[39]

CREATE LONGER WAIT TIMES ALERT!

INS (now USCIS) increases user fees for legal immigrants. As you will see later in this timeline, whenever fees are increased a flood of applications pour in to beat them and the legal immigration backlogs swell. The agency knows this always happens but as you will see the agency has not figured out how to deal with existing backlogs, let alone the new backlog that always follow whenever they increase fees.

• **Adjustment of certain fees of the immigration examinations fee account** [63 FR 43604] [FR 63-98], *Federal Register CITE:* August 14, 1998 via USCIS website. "This rule adjusts the fees schedule of the Immigration Examinations Fee Account (IEFA) for certain immigration adjudication and naturalization applications and petitions."[40]

Clinton era: 1999

CRIME ALERT!

• **INS inspector indicted on bribery counts**—headline, *Associated Press*, June 20, 1999. "LAS CRUCES-A federal grand jury has indicted an Immigration and Naturalization Service inspector on three counts of accepting bribes. Alfred Torres, 48, of Columbus allegedly received bribes in exchange for letting vehicles pass into the United States from Mexico without inspection.[41]

Clinton era: 2000

INCOMPETENCE & BREAK THE LAW ALERT!

• **Source: Government Accountability Office Report:** INS Not Making Timely Deposits of Application Fees, Sep 29, 2000, summary below.[42]

Pursuant to a congressional request, GAO provided information on: (1) extent to which the Immigration and Naturalization Service (INS) made timely deposits of the fees that it collected from aliens who applied for benefits; and (2) potential costs to the government if INS fee deposits were not timely.

GAO noted that: (1) because the *data maintained by INS was not complete*, GAO was unable to fully determine the extent to which INS complied with Department of the Treasury regulations requiring that receipts totaling $5,000 or more be deposited on the same day if they were received prior to the deposit cutoff time, or the next day if they were received too late to meet the cutoff time; (2) *INS maintained initial application acceptance processing data* for its four service centers, which handled about 75 percent of the applications received; (3) however, *INS did not maintain such data* for its 33 district offices, which handled the remaining 25 percent of applications received; (4) in fiscal year 1999, *INS service centers did not generally make timely fee deposits;* (5) whereas Treasury requires that fees totaling $5,000 or more be deposited on the same day or the day after they are received, INS took, on average, at least 12 additional days beyond Treasury's time requirement; (6) GAO estimated that the resulting interest cost to the government, or the cost for interest incurred on debt or other obligations, was about *$640,000 in fiscal year 1999;* (7) *GAO estimates are conservative because GAO did not have data on certain phases of the fee deposit process--such as the amount of time that applications remained unopened* *in service center mailrooms--that may have caused additional delays in the time taken to deposit fees;* (8) any additional delays would have increased the amount of interest cost to the government; and (9) INS' contract of application processing services provided the contractor with more time to make fee deposits *than is allowed by Treasury regulations* [italics mine].

FUN FACT!

When people complain that it is wrong to call illegal aliens—aliens and accuse others of being a racist, heartless or cruel for doing so know this: the U.S. government calls legal immigrants "aliens" every day. We are even given ALIEN status numbers. Oh, the fake outrage you have seen on TV. Who is going to play the race card now?

If you are upset about the use of the word "alien," take it up with the U.S. government then you can apologize to every single LEGAL immigrant if that makes you feel better.

[**Source:** United States Citizenship and Immigration Services[43] Department of Homeland Security[44]]

6 •

PRESIDENT GEORGE W. BUSH ERA

Bush era: 2001

INCOMPETENCE ALERT!

For legal immigrants stuck in a broken, backlogged system incompetence is still an issue at the INS (now USCIS) despite receiving cash infusions (including from increased user fees during Clinton era) and additional staffing. President Clinton hands President George W. Bush a mess. Still wondering why there is an illegal alien problem?

• **Source: Government and Accountability Office Report:** Immigration Benefits: Several Factors Impede Timeliness of Application Processing, May 4, 2001, summary excerpt below.[45]

Congress, the media, and immigrant advocacy groups have criticized the Immigration and Naturalization Service (INS) for its inability to provide immigrants with timely decisions on their applications for such benefits as naturalization and legal permanent residence. INS continues to experience significant problems managing its application workload despite years of increasing budgets and staff. Automation improvements would provide INS with the management information it needs to determine how long aliens have been waiting for their applications to be processed. *Automation improvements would also help INS determine whether it is processing all the applications it receives, working on applications in the order in which they are received, and providing prompt and correct responses to applicants' inquiries about the status of their cases. INS does not know how to maximize the deployment of staff to process applications in a timely fashion because it lacks a systematically developed staff resource allocation model.* Such a model could help INS determine the right number and types of staff it needs, efficiently distribute staff to the right locations, and *ensure that resources are deployed commensurate with the workload to minimize backlogs and processing times.* INS could reduce the need to revoke employment authorization documents by providing guidance and training on application screening to its district staff and taking steps to ascertain whether improvements could be made to the application screening process [italics mine].

Bush era: 2002

NATIONAL SECURITY ALERT!

Who is coming to America? Criminals, drug dealers, terrorists? INS (now the USCIS) acknowledges fraud concerns—criminals exploit an incompetent and inefficient agency.

• **Source: Government and Accountability Office Report:** Immigration Benefit Fraud: Focused Approach Is Needed to Address Problems, Jan 31, 2002, summary below.[46]

Immigration and Naturalization Service (INS) officials believe that some aliens are using the benefit application process to carry out illegal activities, such as crimes of violence, narcotics trafficking, and terrorism. The extent of immigration benefit fraud is unknown, but INS officials and others believe that this problem will increase as smugglers and other criminal enterprises use fraud to bring illegal aliens, including criminals, into the United States. INS investigative units in both the service centers and the district offices investigate possible benefit fraud on the basis of information they receive from staff who process benefit applications, other INS units, the public, and law enforcement agencies. *Providing immigration benefits in a timely manner may conflict with the goal of preserving the integrity of the legal immigration system. Although INS recognizes the need to balance these competing goals, it has not always succeeded.* INS has several performance measures in place to gauge the results of its benefit fraud enforcement activities. However, *INS has not established outcome-based performance measures to assess the results of fraud activities. Additionally, INS has not established goals or measurement criteria for the service center units that are responsible for fraud investigations* [italics mine].

MIND-BENDING INCOMPETENCE & NATIONAL SECURITY ALERT!

Americans were blindsided when they saw the shocking incompetence at the INS (now USCIS). *Do officials even read the applications?!*—something legal immigrants have wondered about even today. America's immigration agency approves two 9/11 hijackers for student visas.

• **Six months after Sept. 11, hijackers' visa approval letters received**—headline, *CNN*, March 13, 2002. "MIAMI, Florida -- Six months to the day after Mohamed Atta and Marwan Al-Shehhi flew planes into the World Trade Center, the Immigration and Naturalization Service notified a Venice, Florida, flight school that the two men had been approved for student visas."[47]

WASHINGTON LEADERSHIP & LAWLESSNESS ALERT!

Congress holds hearings to decide whether or not the INS should be demolished or reformed. Americans finally learn not only about the incompetence but lawlessness at this agency that directly affects national security and the economy. Ultimately Washington decides more money is the solution. Isn't that always their so-called solution? Newsflash: as you will see money is not the solution.

• **What's wrong with the INS? Critics, defenders agree: agency needs overhauling**—headline, *CNN*, March 21, 2002. "Conflicted" doesn't begin to explain the problems at the Immigration and Naturalization Service, but it's a start.

"Local and regional offices feel like they can make and enforce their own policies," he said. "It is unmanageable and has unclear lines of authority. It has turfs, and it's hard for the central office to manage."

The lack of accountability festers, Helton said, because the agency's clients are immigrants, powerless and easily intimidated. "The people it serves have no viable recourse," Helton said.

A former INS commissioner agreed. Wayward regional offices "tend to be the case in any large government agency, and that certainly is the case with the INS," said Doris Meisner, who oversaw the INS from 1993 until 2001 during the Clinton administration.[48]

WASHINGTON LEADERSHIP ALERT!

Instead of shutting down the INS and starting over with new people where the rule of law, accountability and competence matter, the INS is renamed the United States Citizenship and Immigration Services (USCIS) and more money is poured into it. According to President Bush's fiscal 2003 immigration budget the INS (now USCIS) received a five-year, $500-million initiative to reduce wait-times and backlogs. FYI: The agency received an additional $500 million during the Bush administration's last days in office. Today long wait times and backlogs are still a problem.

• **Statement of Eduardo Aguirre Jr., Director of USCIS of DHS on "The President's FY 2005 Budget Request"**—headline, *The Senate Appropriations Committee and Subcommittee on Homeland Security,* March 30, 2004.

"Beginning in FY 2002, the President pledged, and the Congress supported, a multi-year $500 million initiative to attain a universal six-month processing time standard for all immigration benefit applications while providing quality service to all customers. We developed a comprehensive Backlog Elimination Plan prior to September 11, 2001 to achieve this goal. The Plan called for improvements to processes and expanded quality assurance efforts designed to achieve a high level of performance … In FY 2002, processing times for applications averaged, by type, between three and seventy-two months. By the end of the year, these same averages were reduced to between one and twenty-six months. However, September 11, 2001 profoundly affected our business operations, employees, and stakeholders."[49]

• **Immigration to go paperless**—headline, *Washington Post,* November 7, 2008. "If successful, the five-year, $500 million effort to convert U.S. Citizenship and Immigration Services' case-management system from paper-based to electronic could reduce backlogs and processing delays by at least 20 percent, and possibly more than 50 percent, people close to the project said ... Modernization efforts, proposed in 1999, have been delayed by funding problems, inertia, post-Sept. 11 security demands and reorganization triggered by the creation of the Homeland Security Department. The department's inspector general in 2007 faulted the agency for being "entrenched in a cycle of continual planning, with little progress."[50]

Bush era: 2004

ECONOMY ALERT!

Broken immigration contributes to California's economic woes.

• **Illegal aliens cost California billions**, *Washington Times*, December 6, 2004. "Illegal immigration costs the taxpayers of California — which has the highest number of illegal aliens nationwide — $10.5 billion a year for education, health care and incarceration, according to a study released yesterday. A key finding of the report by the Federation for American Immigration Reform (FAIR) said the state's already struggling kindergarten-through-12th-grade education system spends $7.7 billion a year on children of illegal aliens, who constitute 15 percent of the student body. The report also said the incarceration of convicted illegal aliens in state prisons and jails and uncompensated medical outlays for health care provided to illegal aliens each amounted to about $1.4 billion annually. The incarceration costs did not include judicial expenditures or the monetary costs of the crimes committed by illegal aliens that led to their incarceration."[51]

INCOMPETENCE ALERT!

It's still Vegas-like for legal immigrants. Backlogs continue to balloon, some applications are processed while others are lost or stored for years because the agency still does not keep track of them. Under Bush, "backlog elimination centers" are opened up around the country in an attempt to clear backlogs—*by getting rid of legal immigrants stuck in them* ... there are 6.2 million pending applications in 2003.[52] Agency receives even more money.

• Source: Government and Accountability Office Report: Immigration Application Fees, Current Fees Are Not Sufficient to Fund U.S. Citizenship and Immigration Services' Operations, Jan 5, 2004, summary excerpt below.[53]

The Homeland Security Act of 2002 (HSA) established the Bureau of Citizenship and Immigration Services (CIS) within the Department of Homeland Security (DHS).

We determined that fees were not sufficient to fully fund CIS's operations. In part, this has resulted because (1) the current fee schedule is based on an outdated fee study that did not include all costs of CIS's operations and (2) costs have increased since that study was completed due to an additional processing requirement and other actions. *While it is clear fees are insufficient to fully fund CIS's operations, there is insufficient cost data to determine the full extent of the shortfall. A fundamental problem is that CIS does not have a system to track the status of each application as it moves through the process. Accordingly, CIS does not have information on the extent to which work on applications in process remains to be finished. In addition, CIS does not know the current cost of each step to process each application. The effect is that CIS knows neither the cost to process new applications nor the cost to complete pending applications.*

Further, because DHS is still determining how administrative and overhead functions will be carried out and the related costs allocated, CIS does not know what future administrative and overhead costs will be. For the 3-year period from fiscal year 2001 through 2003, *CIS's reported operating costs exceeded available fees by almost $460 million, thus creating the need for appropriated funds. CIS projects that this situation will remain in fiscal year 2004. Since the beginning of fiscal year 2001, the number of pending applications increased by more than 2.3 million (about 59 percent) to about 6.2 million at the end of fiscal year 2003. This increase occurred despite additional appropriations beginning in fiscal year 2002 of $80 million annually to address the backlog. In addition, CIS has not performed an analysis of the steps needed to reduce processing times to the 6-month average goal established in the President's backlog initiative. These times increased significantly in fiscal year 2003 to levels well above the 6-month target established in CIS's March 2002 Backlog Elimination Plan. Absent actions to increase fees, reduce* *processing costs and times, or both, as well as to improve the timeliness and completeness of fee schedule updates, CIS will continue to need appropriated funds to avoid even greater increases in the backlog of pending applications. The full costs of CIS's operations cannot be determined until analyses of the costs to process incoming and pending applications and administrative and overhead costs are completed* [italics mine].

FAILED GOVERNMENT LEADERSHIP & NATIONAL SECURITY ALERT!

In June 2004 Congress holds a subcommittee on immigration and border security called: Families and businesses in limbo: the detrimental impact of the immigration backlog.[54] Blah, blah, blah … yes, legal immigrants know this. It is true. Unfortunately almost a decade later the backlogs and the same problems exist today.

• Excerpt opening statement: "Today, the Subcommittee on Immigration, Border Security, and Claims will examine a quite different subject from our last oversight hearing. Instead of reviewing the tools needed to combat illegal human smuggling into the United States, we will examine the plight of those legal immigrants working through the immigration and petition process and those seeking to naturalize. Those aliens who follow the law and dutifully apply for immigration status with U.S. Citizenship and Immigration Services, or USCIS, should not be stranded in legal limbo while waiting for the 6.2 million petition backlog to be cleared. This is especially the case for those patiently waiting abroad for their legitimate immigration applications to be approved. Some families have been kept apart as alien relatives abroad have had to wait for USCIS to adjudicate the petition paperwork. In some cases, petitions sit in a pile for literally years, and applicants must periodically refile certain items, like fingerprints, as they expire. And when I talk about expiring, I mean the applications, not the applicants.

American companies have also suffered. American multinationals file papers with USCIS to bring employees from abroad or to hire graduates of American universities. One must ask what incentive there is for aliens abroad to make legal applications for entry only to wait lengthy periods in the backlog.

The immigration backlog also harms our national security. A recent General Accounting Office study describes how poor visa overstay tracking complicates efforts to ensure domestic security. Indeed, we have seen how 9/11 terrorists took advantage of backlogs, workload, and poor record checks to remain undetected and undisturbed in the U.S. A recent Nixon Center study indicates that the al Qaeda terrorist network has used and continues its strategies of using national immigration systems to place operatives. In fact, 7 percent of all applications processed result in an initial security or criminal hit of some sort. But if checks are not processed for years, dangerous aliens may roam free in our communities here in the United States."

Bush era: 2005

INCOMPETENCE ALERT!
Life for legal immigrants at the mercy of faceless bureaucrats includes ineptitude with basic phone calls compounded by the agency's inability to provide accurate information.

• **Source: Government and Accountability Office Report:** Immigration Services: Better Contracting Practices Needed at Call Centers, Jun 30, 2005, summary excerpt below.[55]

The U.S. Citizenship and Immigration Services (USCIS) bureau within the Department of Homeland Security (DHS) provides toll-free telephone assistance through call centers to immigrants, their attorneys, and others seeking information about U.S. immigration services and benefits. *As the volume of calls increased--from about 13 million calls in fiscal year 2002 to about 21 million calls in fiscal year 2004--questions were raised about USCIS's ability to ensure the reliability and accuracy of the information provided at call centers run by an independent contractor.* This report analyzes: (1) the performance measures established by USCIS to monitor and evaluate the performance of contractor-operated call centers; (2) how performance measures were used to evaluate the contractor's performance; and (3) any actions USCIS has taken, or plans to take, to strengthen call center operations.

USCIS developed seven performance measures intended to assess the performance and overall quality of responses provided by customer service representatives at contractor-operated call centers. These measures include how quickly calls were answered and the accuracy of information provided. The contract between USCIS and its contractor stipulated that the contractor could earn financial incentive awards if the average monthly performance met or exceeded the standards on a quarterly basis at each of four call centers. *Conversely, financial deductions could be made if the standards were not met. USCIS did not finalize the terms regarding how the contractor's actual performance would be calculated, or scored, before awarding the contract. This limited USCIS's ability to exercise performance incentives (positive or negative) because the parties could not reach agreement on performance terms. USCIS suspended the use of financial incentives while the parties negotiated the issue. Agreement was not reached after 16 months, however, USCIS determined that the contractor had failed to meet standards for 4 of the 7 performance measures in the fourth quarter of 2004 and took action to reduce its payments for services. The contractor objected, citing the lack of agreement on the performance measurements and the impact of workload increases, but USCIS disagreed and stated it would reduce payment. In a separate but related matter, USCIS failed to meet contractual, regulatory, and GAO standards pertaining to how the contractor's performance would be documented--especially with respect to any deficiencies* [italics mine].

September 2005

NATIONAL SECURITY ALERT!

Terrorists are still exploiting a broken immigration system.

• **Immigration and Terrorism: Moving Beyond the 9/11 Staff Report on Terrorist Travel**—headline, *Center for Immigration,* 2005.[56]

Among the findings:

- Of the 94 foreign-born terrorists who operated in the United States, the study found that about two-thirds (59) committed immigration fraud prior to or in conjunction with taking part in terrorist activity.
- Of the 59 terrorists who violated the law, many committed multiple immigration violations -- 79 instances in all.

- In 47 instances, immigration benefits sought or acquired prior to 9/11 enabled the terrorists to stay in the United States after 9/11 and continue their terrorist activities. In at least two instances, terrorists were still able to acquire immigration benefits after 9/11.
- Temporary visas were a common means of entering; 18 terrorists had student visas and another four had applications approved to study in the United States. At least 17 terrorists used a visitor visa -- either tourist (B2) or business (B1).
- There were 11 instances of passport fraud and 10 instances of visa fraud; in total 34 individuals were charged with making false statements to an immigration official.
- In at least 13 instances, terrorists overstayed their temporary visas.
- In 17 instances, terrorists claimed to lack proper travel documents and applied for asylum, often at a port of entry.
- Fraud was used not only to gain entry into the United States, but also to remain, or "embed," in the country.
- Seven terrorists were indicted for acquiring or using various forms of fake identification, including driver's licenses, birth certificates, Social Security cards, and immigration arrival records.
- Once in the United States, 16 of 23 terrorists became legal permanent residents, often by marrying an American. There were at least nine sham marriages.
- In total, 20 of 21 foreign terrorists became naturalized U.S. citizens.
-

Bush era: 2006

INCOMPETENCE & NATIONAL SECURITY ALERT!

More on why legal immigration is a nifty sound bite for politicians but it can be a devastating heart-wrenching exercise in futility for legal immigrants. Sleepless nights, stress, worries and endless lawyer bills ... the agency is still losing files. Meanwhile the USCIS approves a man linked to Hezbollah.

• **Citizenship agency (USCIS) lost 111,000 files**—headline, *Washington Post,* November 29, 2006. "U.S. Citizenship and Immigration Services has lost track of 111,000 files in 14 of the agency's busiest district offices and processed as many as 30,000 citizenship applications last year without the necessary files, congressional investigators reported yesterday. The Government Accountability Office, Congress's audit arm, conducted the review at the request of Sens. Charles E. Grassley (R-Iowa) and Susan Collins (R-Maine) after U.S. authorities granted citizenship in 2002 to a man without checking his primary file. The file, which was lost, indicated ties to the militant Islamic group Hezbollah.[57]

CRIME & CORRUPTION ALERT!

There are serious fraud challenges for the U.S. Immigration and Customs Enforcement (ICE) to verify employment eligibility. Corruption is an issue within and outside the exploitable agency.

• **Source: Government and Accountability Office Report:** Immigration Enforcement: Weaknesses Hinder Employment Verification and Worksite Enforcement Efforts, Jun 19, 2006, summary below.[58]

The opportunity for employment is one of the most important magnets attracting illegal immigrants to the United States. The Immigration Reform and Control Act (IRCA) of 1986 established an employment eligibility verification process and a sanctions program for fining employers for noncompliance. *Few modifications have been made to the verification process and sanctions program since 1986, and immigration experts state that a more reliable verification process and a strengthened worksite enforcement capacity are needed to help deter illegal immigration.* This testimony is based on GAO's August 2005 report on the employment verification process and worksite enforcement efforts. In this testimony, GAO provides observations on (1) the current employment verification process and (2) U.S. Immigration and Customs Enforcement's (ICE) priorities and resources for the worksite enforcement program and the challenges it faces in implementing that program.

The current employment verification (Form I-9) process is based on employers' review of documents presented by new employees to prove their identity and work eligibility. On the Form I-9, employers certify that they have reviewed documents presented by their employees and that the documents appear genuine and relate to the individual presenting the documents. *However, document fraud (use of counterfeit documents) and identity fraud (fraudulent use of valid documents or information belonging to others) have undermined the employment verification process by making it difficult for employers who want to comply with the process to ensure they hire only authorized workers and easier for unscrupulous employers to knowingly hire unauthorized workers with little fear of sanction. In addition, the large number and variety of documents acceptable for proving work eligibility has hindered employer verification efforts.* In 1998, the former Immigration and Naturalization Service (INS), now part of DHS, proposed revising the Form I-9 process, particularly to reduce the number of acceptable work eligibility documents, *but DHS has not yet finalized the proposal.* The Basic Pilot Program, a voluntary program through which participating employers electronically verify employees' work eligibility, shows promise to enhance the current employment verification process, help reduce document fraud, and assist ICE in better targeting its worksite enforcement efforts. *Yet, several weaknesses in the pilot program's implementation, such as its inability to detect identity fraud and DHS delays in entering data into its databases, could adversely affect increased use of the pilot program, if not addressed.* The worksite enforcement program has been a relatively low priority under both INS and ICE. Consistent with the DHS mission to combat terrorism, after September 11, 2001, INS and then ICE focused worksite enforcement efforts mainly on detecting and removing unauthorized workers from critical infrastructure sites. *Since fiscal year 1999, the numbers of employer notices of intent to fine and administrative worksite arrests have generally declined. According to ICE, this decline is due to various factors, such as the prevalence of document fraud that makes it difficult to prove employer violations. ICE officials told us that the agency has previously experienced difficulties in proving employer violations and setting and collecting fine amounts that meaningfully deter employers from knowingly hiring unauthorized workers. In April 2006, ICE announced a new interior enforcement strategy to target employers who knowingly hire unauthorized workers by bringing criminal charges against them, and ICE has reported increases in the number of criminal arrests and indictments since fiscal year 2004.* However, it is too early to tell what effect, if any, this new strategy will have on enhancing worksite enforcement efforts and identifying unauthorized workers and their employers [italics mine].

CRIME & CORRUPTION ALERT!

• **Cash, cars, jewelry: Some corruption cases involving immigration officers**—headline, *Associated Press,* September 24, 2006.[59] "In the past 12 months, dozens of U.S. immigration employees have been accused of corruption-related charges." Below are some cases, drawn from a review of court records and government announcements:

• Robert Schofield, a USCIS district office supervisor in Fairfax, Va., was arrested in June, accused of illegally granting residency and issuing naturalization certificates to more than 100 unqualified immigrants. Qiming Ye, a Chinese citizen, also was charged for allegedly brokering deals between Schofield and Asian immigrants. One unqualified immigrant was granted residency status after meeting Schofield's wife in the Philippines, and then living with Schofield and baby-sitting his stepchild for a year, a court affidavit alleges. When stopped by Customs officials at an airport, the immigrant provided Schofield's name, cellphone and home telephone number from memory, the affidavit said. Passports seized from Ye's residence included green card stamps bearing Schofield's ID, and phone traces showed dozens of calls between Ye and Schofield's home number and his Department of Homeland Security cellphone, the court documents allege. "Numerous" allegations of bribery involving Schofield have been reported in the last decade, an investigator said in an affidavit. A trial date is pending.

• Phillip Browne, a district adjudication officer for USCIS in Manhattan, was indicted in May on charges of visa fraud and money laundering. Prosecutors contend he conspired with his sister and others to provide hundreds of residency papers, or green cards, in a sham marriage scheme that netted more than $1 million. The operation allegedly ran for at least 4½ years. According to prosecutors, Browne's sister ran a business that claimed to offer customers financial and legal help. Instead, prosecutors allege, the business provided fraudulent green cards for fees ranging from $8,000 to $16,000. Browne's sister allegedly paid U.S. citizens to enter into sham marriages with her clients, or produced phony documentation indicating a marriage to an American had already occurred. Based upon the sham marriages, immigrant clients then submitted green card applications, which were allegedly approved by Browne. In all, 30 people were charged. A trial date is pending.

• Robert Walton, an immigration employee for 20 years, was sentenced in April to a year in prison for approving citizenship and residency for immigrants who did not meet requirements. Prosecutors alleged that Walton accepted gifts—a diamond earring, a gold and diamond bracelet, and $5,000—for approving applications. Walton said in a letter to the judge that the money was a loan and the jewelry pieces were not bribes but thank-you gifts. Walton, who previously worked as a border inspector, intelligence officer and supervisory inspector, said he sought the immigration adjudicator's position because he was "burned out" and wanted a regular Monday-Friday job. He insisted his actions were due to lack of training.

"The job ... had no Standard Operating Procedures, written or verbal," he wrote.

"I worked for my government for 18 years before I was given any direction in ethics," wrote Walton, a church deacon, who added he eventually received a book on the subject. One   person   who provided jewelry to Walton was convicted in a separate case of bribing another Detroit-area immigration officer for help in illegally bringing immigrants to America from Lebanon. That officer, Janice Halstead, was sentenced in 2004 to two years in prison for supplying documents that allowed some 130 migrants from Yemen and Lebanon into the country."[60]

• **Immigration Official Pleads Guilty to Falsifying Documents**—headline, *Washington Post*, December 1, 2006. "A Department of Homeland Security supervisor pleaded guilty... to pocketing more than $600,000 in bribes."[61]

PLAYING POLITICS WITH IMMIGRATION ALERT!

On June 7, 2006, President George Bush signed Executive Order 13404 creating the Task Force on New Americans.[62] In short it is an immigrant outreach and integration program that is similar to President Clinton's CUSA program (and later becomes President Obama's Citizenship Grant Program) where Green Card holders receive help (your tax dollars at work) to become citizens with the right to vote. More on this in Obama era.

Executive Order 13404 article excerpt and link: The "Task Force on New Americans" to intended to "strengthen the efforts of the Department of Homeland Security (DHS) and Federal, State, and local agencies to help legal immigrants embrace the common core of American civic culture, learn our common language, and fully become Americans." The following federal departments were included in Bush's order: DHS, State, Treasury, Defense, Justice, Agriculture, Commerce, Labor, Health and Human Services, Housing and Urban Development, and Education.

The New American Task Force was ordered, in part, to: "provide direction [to legal immigrants] ... concerning the integration into American society... particularly through instruction in English, civics, and history ...." Funding was determined by the Secretary of the DHS.[63]

WHISTLEBLOWER & CORRUPTION ALERT!

• **Whistleblower: Immigration Penetrated, Corrupt**—headline, *Newsmax,* June 14, 2006. "WASHINGTON—The U.S. immigration system is so broken that it can't be fixed, a former top security official at the Department of Homeland Security's Citizenship and Immigration Services (CIS) told *NewsMax* in an exclusive interview.[64]

"Internal corruption at CIS is so pervasive that hostile foreign governments have penetrated the agency," said Michael J. Maxwell, who was *forced to resign as chief of the CIS Office of Security and Investigation* earlier this year.

"Terrorists and organized crime are gaming the immigration system with impunity. Taken together, these three elements form the perfect storm," Maxwell said.

"You can't separate immigration from national security, and that's what keeps me up at night," he added. The Department of Homeland Security has begun to take Maxwell's warnings seriously. A just-released report from the DHS Office of Inspector General revealed that *45,008 aliens from countries on the U.S. list of state-sponsors of terror (SST) or from countries that protected terrorist organizations and their members were released into the general public between 2001 and 2005, even though immigration officers couldn't confirm their identities.*

Even worse, the report states: "it is not known exactly how many of these . . . aliens were ultimately issued final orders of removal and actually removed, since such data is not tracked" by the Detention and Removal Office of Immigration and Customs Enforcement (ICE)."

Bush era: 2007

INCOMPETENCE & FAILED POLICY ALERT!

The USCIS gets even more money. The agency increases fees for legal immigrants by 86%. Backlogs and delays for legal immigrants explode—again. Incompetence remains an issue. Outdated quotas and flawed policies play a big role here too. The report below is dated 2009 but it addresses the 2007 fee increases. With all that additional money the problems at the USCIS continue. Are you still wondering why there is an illegal alien problem?

• **Source: Government and Accountability Office Report:** Federal User Fees: Additional Analyses and Timely Review s Could Improve Immigration and Naturalization User Fee Design and USCIS operations, January 23, 2009, one GAO recommendation is still outstanding today, summary below.[65]

U.S. Citizenship and Immigration Services (USCIS) announced an increase to its immigration and naturalization application fees by an average of 86 percent, effective July 2007, contributing to a surge in application volume that challenged the agency's pre-adjudicative operations. In July 2007, the incoming application volume increased an unprecedented 100 percent over the prior month and the processing of 1.47 million applications was delayed. GAO was asked to review USCIS's current fee design and compare it to the principles in GAO's user-fee design guide and USCIS's management of operations affected by the new fees, specifically in projecting application volumes and contracting for application processing services. To do so, GAO reviewed legislation and agency documentation; compared the fee design to GAO's principles of effective user-fee design (equity, efficiency, revenue adequacy, and administrative burden); visited processing centers; and interviewed agency officials at these locations and in headquarters.

USCIS's 2007 fee design reflects choices and trade-offs consistent with several of GAO's four user-fee design dimensions-- efficiency, equity, revenue adequacy, and administrative burden. For example, in three areas the fee design reflects policy choices related to equity and administrative burden considerations: (1) the structure of fee exemptions and waivers, (2) limitations on certain fee increases for a population deemed unlikely to be able to pay, and (3) decisions about how costs were assigned among users. *However, USCIS did not conduct the analyses necessary to fully inform congressional decision-making or internal deliberations on some key areas, such as the cost of activities funded by fees whose rates are set in statute. Notably, the $1,000 fee for USCIS's premium-processing service for employment-based applications, which was the fifth largest single generator of funds for USCIS in fiscal year 2007, will be used for business process and technology improvements. As such, the additional costs of premium processing services are funded by nonpremium processing fee-paying applicants, raising equity concerns. Since USCIS has not identified the total costs of these services, the actual dollar amount being subsidized is unknown. The new fee design also does not allow for an appropriate "reserve" or carryover balance, to ensure the continuity of operations and cover fixed costs in the event of a decrease in applications, nor does it consider the costs associated with certain fee collection operations. According to USCIS's schedule, if the next review identifies a needed fee adjustment, it would occur in September 2009. However, USCIS did not provide documentation that would allow us to determine whether the 2009 fee review would address identified shortcomings in the 2007 fee review or whether the remaining time frames for key milestones, such as refining data and the proposed rulemaking schedule, are reasonable. Absent timely reviews, it is more likely that fees and costs will become misaligned, leading to costly challenges.* Projections of USCIS application volume have historically been developed and used as budget tools but do not effectively inform workload management efforts. Specifically, the projections do not identify monthly variations in application volume, despite variations that regularly exceed 20 percent and the serious operational challenges associated with application surges. *USCIS's contractors do not receive workload* *projection information, despite requirements that processing centers shall maintain the capacity to accommodate "spikes" in receipt volumes that are anticipated at least 45 to 90 calendar days in advance. Further, USCIS projection documents do not consistently record critical information such as factors that drive application volume, inhibiting analysis that could improve projections over time. Service-center contractors process USCIS mail and are paid according to a fixed unit price per piece. Contractors count up to 90 percent of incoming mail, but USCIS has not developed an agency wide standard operating procedure for validating the contractors' counts. As a result, USCIS is limited in its ability to verify that USCIS is receiving the service that it is paying for* [italics mine].

COMPREHENSIVE IMMIGRATION REFORM & HYPOCRISY ALERT!

President Bush with Senator Ted Kennedy (D-MA) and a bi-partisan group of senators—this time the "Gang of Twelve" try to pass Comprehensive Immigration Reform that included a path to citizenship for 12 million illegal aliens while slapping all legal immigrants from around the world in the face. It fails. Then Senator Barack Obama voted against it but now he is for it.[66] But don't worry; thanks to lawmakers the USCIS has received hundreds of millions of dollars to modernize … oops, as you will see the agency is still having serious problems today.[67]

CRIME ALERT!

• **U.S. agents accused of aiding Islamist scheme**—headline, *Washington Times,* August 15, 2007. "A criminal investigations report says several USCIS employees are accused of aiding Islamic extremists with identification fraud and of exploiting the visa system for personal gain. The confidential 2006 USCIS report said that despite the severity of the potential security breaches, most are not investigated "due to lack of resources."[68]
• Bribery—cash, gifts or sex is but one criminal element at America's immigration agency. There are others like embezzlement and abuse of public trust. In the **United States of America v. Catherine Ileen Spear,** (June 26, 2007), for instance, according to the indictment, "Catherine Spear worked as a federal immigration employee

responsible for the intake of applications submitted by persons applying for changes in their immigration status. Instead of processing the applications, she kept the fees accompanying the applications and then threw the applications in the trash."[69]

PLAYING POLITICS WITH IMMIGRATION ALERT?!

Senator Barack Obama and Rep Luis Gutierrez (D-IL) introduce the Citizenship Promotion Act of 2007, S795 (reminiscent to the Clinton's CUSA program and Bush's New American Task Force Executive Order). The bill would have given $80 million to community organizers to 'organize' the immigrant community to become citizens (then they can vote).[70] Free English classes and lunch!!! It reduced fees (subsidized by taxpayers) and weakened background checks by speeding them up. Naturally the bill would add to USCIS's ubiquitous backlogs. It is dead now but as you will see in *Chapter 10: Game Changer* the policy is being enacted through other channels—13 federal agencies!

DISHONEST POLITICIANS ALERT:

When politicians say today that the immigration system needs to be modernized know this: Congress already provided USCIS in 2007 with $181,990,000 in appropriations to transform and modernize the system. Following is a GAO report that was released in 2012 but refers back to the 2007 funding. As you will see in the Obama Era Chapter, after receiving almost a $1 billion to modernize the USCIS still does not operate using "best practices," is running behind schedule and over budget. Do not be deceived. How many millions in appropriations/funding are we up to? Lost count.

• **Source: Government Accountability Office Report**: Managing for Results A Guide for Using the GPRA Modernization Act to Help Inform Congressional Decision Making, June 2012, p. 15-16.[71]

USCIS, a component of the Department of Homeland Security (DHS), adjudicates benefits requests and petitions for individuals seeking to become citizens of the United States or to study, live, or work in this country. Our past work, and that of the DHS Office of Inspector General (OIG), has identified performance challenges USCIS faces in processing benefits. For example, a 2005 DHS OIG report found that USCIS's ability to annually process more than 7 million benefit applications has been hindered by inefficient, paper-based processes, resulting in a backlog that peaked in 2004 at more than 3.8 million cases. Recognizing that dependence on paper files makes it difficult to process immigration benefits efficiently, USCIS began a transformation initiative in 2005 to transition to electronic processing to enhance customer service, improve efficiency, and prevent future backlogs of immigration benefit applications.

Recognizing the importance of this *transformation initiative, Congress provided USCIS with $181,990,000 in appropriations in fiscal year 2007, which included, according to the Conference Committee report, $47 million to upgrade its information technology and business systems.* However, before USCIS could obligate this funding, Congress directed the agency to submit a strategic transformation plan and expenditure plan with details on expected performance and deliverables. Congress also directed us to review and report to the appropriations committees on the plans. According to a House Committee on Appropriations report that accompanied the act, the committee wanted to ensure that USCIS's transformation efforts were consistent with best practices. In May 2007, USCIS submitted its Transformation Program Strategic Plan and Expenditure Plan to the appropriations committees. We briefed the committees in June and July 2007 on our review, which found that USCIS's plans had mixed success in addressing key practices for organizational transformations. *As illustrated in table 1, more than half of the key practices (five out of nine) were either partially or not addressed. Our report noted that more attention was needed in a number of management-related activities, including performance measurement* [italics mine].

INCOMPETENCE ALERT!

Congressman Zoe Lofgren's sounds the alarm on the continued incompetence of USCIS.

• In a July 30, 2007, press release Lofgren's office said, "USCIS has consistently failed to reduce application backlogs and has suffered from a lack of transparency and effective management... 'After repeated requests over several months, USCIS has yet to provide Congress with a detailed plan.'"[72]

Bush era: 2008:

INCOMPETENCE ALERT!

More on why legal immigration is still Vegas-like and a heart wrenching exercise in futility for countless legal immigrants living at the mercy of faceless bureaucrats. The agency is still losing files and wasting taxpayer dollars. If legal immigrants cannot get processed is it still a mystery why America has an illegal alien/undocumented worker problem?

• **Immigration to go paperless: Agency plans electronic overhaul of case-management system,** *Washington Post*—headline, November 7, 2008. "Government investigators have reported that the [USCIS'] pre-computer-age paper filing system incurs $100 million a year in archiving, storage, retrieval and shipping costs; has led to the loss or misplacement of more than 100,000 files; and has contributed to backlogs and delays **for millions of cases."**[73]

CRIME, CORRUPTION & SEX ALERT!

• **An agent, a green card, and a demand for sex**—headline, *New York Times*, March 21, 2008. A USCIS adjudicator was arrested after he was caught on tape, telling a 22-year old Colombian woman, "I want sex," he said… "You get your green card."[74]
• **Federal agency worker (Hashukh C. Patel, a business interface representative for USCIS and former USCIS adjudication officer) & wife assisted aliens in obtaining visas and shielding them from detection**—indictment, *Department of Justice, Northern District of Georgia,* May 2008. The indictment… charges both defendants with conspiracy to encourage … aliens to come to the U.S. [illegally] for the Patels' private financial gain."[75]

NO TRAVEL ALERT!

It's not only undocumented workers who have to worry if they leave the USA if they can get back in. The same applies to legal immigrants, who followed the laws and did everything correctly while they are stuck in the backlogs waiting to be processed.

Imagine if you found out that your mother was dying and wanted to be with her before she passed and needed to travel internationally. A faceless bureaucrat will tell the legal immigrant that they can go but that doesn't mean they will get back into America. What would you do? Where are the bleeding hearts and the churches now?

• **Top homeland security official accused of hiring illegal immigrants to clean her house**— headline, *Associated Press*, December 5, 2008. "Even warning her not to leave the country 'cause once you leave, you will never be back.'"[76]

LAWLESSNESS ALERT!

As you will see in the GAO report below this arbitrary lawlessness in the immigration court system (funded by taxpayers, not legal immigrants and obviously not illegal aliens either) is not isolated to asylum applications. It has worsened since the Obama administration issued an ICE memo that directs arbitrary prosecutorial discretion when it comes to deportations. More on the ICE Memo and fallout in *Chapter 13: President Obama era, Part II.*

• **Source: Government and Accountability Office Report:** U.S. Asylum System, Significant Variation Existed in Asylum Outcomes across Immigration Courts and Judges, Sep 25, 2008, summary below.[77]

Each year, tens of thousands of people who have been persecuted or fear persecution in their home countries apply for asylum in the United States. Immigration judges (IJ) from the Department of Justice's (DOJ) Executive Office for Immigration Review (EOIR) decide whether to grant or deny asylum to aliens in removal proceedings. Those denied asylum may appeal their case to EOIR's Board of Immigration Appeals (BIA). GAO was asked to assess the variability of IJ rulings, and the effects of policy changes related to appeals and claims. *This report addresses: (1) factors affecting variability in asylum outcomes;* (2) EOIR actions to assist applicants and IJs; (3) *effects associated with procedural changes at the BIA; and* (4) effects of the requirement that asylum seekers apply within 1 year of entering the country. GAO analyzed DOJ asylum data for fiscal years 1995 through mid-2007, visited 5 immigration courts in 3 cities, including those with 3 of the top 4 asylum caseloads; observed asylum hearings; and interviewed key officials. Results of the visits provided additional information but were not projectable.

In the 19 immigration courts that handled almost 90 percent of asylum cases from October 1994 through April 2007, nine factors affected variability in asylum outcomes: (1) filed affirmatively (originally with DHS at his/her own initiative) or defensively (with DOJ, if in removal proceedings); (2) applicant's nationality; (3) time period of the asylum decision; (4) representation; (5) applied within 1 year of entry to the United States; (6) claimed dependents on the application; (7) had ever been detained (defensive cases only); *(8) gender of the immigration judge and (9) length of experience as an immigration judge. After statistically controlling for these factors, disparities across immigration courts and judges existed. For example, affirmative applicants in San Francisco were still 12 times more likely than those in Atlanta to be granted asylum. Further, in 14 of 19 immigration courts for affirmative cases, and 13 of 19 for defensive cases, applicants were at least 4 times more likely to be granted asylum if their cases were decided by the judge with the highest versus the lowest likelihood of granting asylum in that court.* EOIR expanded its programs designed to assist applicants with obtaining representation and has attempted to improve the capabilities of some IJs. EOIR has conducted two grant rate studies and was using information on IJs with unusually high or low grant rates, together with other indicators of IJ performance, to identify IJs who might benefit from additional training and supervision. *However, EOIR lacked the expertise to statistically control for factors that could affect asylum outcomes, and this limited the completeness, accuracy, and usefulness of grant rate information. Without such information, to be used in conjunction with other performance indicators, EOIR's ability to identify IJs who may need additional training and supervision was hindered. EOIR assigned some IJ supervisors to field locations to improve oversight of immigration courts, but EOIR has not determined how many supervisors it needs to effectively supervise IJs and has not provided supervisors with guidance on how to carry out their supervisory role.* Following streamlining (procedural changes) at the BIA in March 2002, BIA's appeals backlog decreased, as did the number of decisions favoring asylum seekers. Such decisions were more than 50 percent lower in the 4 years after streamlining compared to 4 years prior. The authority to affirm the IJ's' decisions without writing an opinion was used in 44 percent of BIA's asylum decisions. In June 2008, EOIR proposed regulatory changes to the streamlining rules, but it is too soon to tell how they will affect appeals outcomes. Data limitations prevented GAO from determining the (1) effect of the 1-year rule on fraudulent applications and denials and (2) resources adjudicators have spent addressing related issues. *EOIR lacked measures of fraud, data on whether the 1-year rule was the basis for asylum denials, and records of time spent addressing such issues. Congress would need to direct EOIR to develop a cost-effective method of collecting data to determine the effect of the rule* [italics mine].

7.

USCIS ATTACKS

The United States Citizenship and Immigration Services (USCIS) has a network of 250 Field Offices, Application Support Centers, Service Centers, the National Benefits Center, Asylum Offices, the National Customer Service Center, and Forms Centers around the country.

The agency is tasked to protect national security by keeping bad guys out. The agency's responsibilities also include employment authorization, advance parole, granting visas, residency, citizenship, adjustment of status, asylum, and refugee status to law abiding foreign-born workers while balancing economic needs and honoring America's tradition as a nation of immigrants.

That said, Washington bureaucrats absolutely loath it when journalists shine a bright light on troubles within their agency and that includes those at the USCIS.

In 2009, for instance, one of my articles reporting on some of the crime and corruption at the USCIS caught the eye of then USCIS Acting Deputy Director Michael Aytes.

In turn, he wrote a scathing letter to the editor of *Canada Free Press* where my article was published defending the indefensible. Below is his letter followed by my response. After reading this book, you will see that the same critical issues I reported on in 2009, (and after the USCIS received hundreds of millions of dollars, still apply today.[78]

Four years later, Michael Ayes has still not responded to my open interview request. Original letter appears in the appendix.

Jan. 23, 2009
Canada Free Press
www.canadafreepress.com
Editor:

U. S. Citizenship and Immigration Services (USCIS) employees are some of the most experienced and highly skilled members of America's federal workforce. As the gatekeepers of the United States' immigration system, we all serve on the front lines of our homeland defense. And we, as any other organization with thousands of employees, are a reflection of our society and are not immune from instances when a few choose to abuse the authority entrusted in them. Your readers have a right to know – and you have a responsibility to report – how our agency deals with those few.

Unfortunately, your online paper chose to run an article on January 21 filled with errors and unsubstantiated information. Worse, it basically labeled this superb organization as one inhabited by "crooks and thugs." As an Immigration Officer with more than 30 years experience [sic] at both the former Immigration and Naturalization Service and USCIS, I simply cannot allow this story to stand.

Ensuring the integrity of the U.S. immigration system is our highest priority. When an individual fails to meet our high standards we work hard to ensure that justice is done, with appropriate and full punishment. That's the record. To further this important mission, USCIS established the Office of Security and Integrity (OSI) in 2007. In doing so, we tripled the resources dedicated to this critical mission and placed it under our executive leadership.

Through OSI's efforts, USCIS is well positioned to evaluate vulnerabilities, expose instances of corruption and create agency controls that minimize the effect a corrupt individual can have on our agency. OSI has also expanded its Investigations Division to receive complaints of alleged employee misconduct, corruption and fraud. We have in place an aggressive program that ensures employees know they are responsible for ensuring our agency's integrity.

Further, the article's accusation that "USCIS is overwhelmed by backlogs from immigrants following America's laws stuck in the nonsensical and degrading bureaucracy," ignores the fact that USCIS received nearly five million applications and petitions for immigrant benefits last year, yet we completed more than six and a half million cases. This substantially reduced processing times – especially for naturalization.

I don't expect someone with very limited knowledge of the U.S. immigration system to be able to offer substantive or constructive criticism of agency policy and procedure. However, I do expect a reporter to stick to the facts and refrain from offering editorial opinion in their work. This article served no other functional purpose other than to tarnish the honorable reputation of our employees and associate the entire USCIS workforce with criminals. It was shameful reporting and a deliberate smear that should not be counted as news.

At USCIS, we can't afford to make mistakes in our work. I challenge your paper to live up to these same high standards and seek to correct the inaccuracies of your story.

Sincerely,

Michael Aytes
Acting Deputy Director
U.S. Citizenship and Immigration Services

My response to USCIS Michael Aytes:

On January 24, 2009 Acting Deputy Director Michael Aytes,[79] currently the highest ranking official at the U.S. Citizenship and Immigration Services (USCIS), sent a scathing letter to *CFP's* editor to rebuke an article I wrote on January 21 entitled, "Crime and Corruption at the UCSIS."[80] My article cited criminal investigations like this one where "several USCIS employees" were "accused of aiding Islamic extremists with identification fraud and of exploiting the visa system for personal gain" as source material.[81] "It was shameful reporting and a deliberate smear that should not be counted as news," Aytes wrote, defending the USCIS, an agency he describes as a "superb organization." He claimed my "article served no other functional purpose other than to tarnish the honorable reputation of our employees and associate the entire USCIS workforce with criminals." He also claimed that my article was full of "errors" and "inaccuracies," however he did not cite the errors, or the alleged "inaccuracies." To attack and smear a journalist's credibility, particularly one who saw the crime and corruption up close and reported it to authorities leading to the conviction of two federal officials for taking cash bribes in exchange for American passports that incidentally launched an international manhunt is outrageous.

I think I must have struck a nerve.

Welcome to the dark inner intrigue at the USCIS, formerly the Immigration Nationalization Services that some people in government (not all) don't want the public to know about. Contrary to Aytes' assertion that my article "should not be counted as news," Americans and the law abiding immigrants who fund the lion's share of this agency's $2.6 billion annual budget through user fees have the right to know what's been going on there. Like a giant Ponzi scheme, the user fees feed the USCIS' bureaucracy and the agency's troubling backlogs because it accepts more immigration applications than it processes.

To begin, it is precisely for the honorable USCIS employees and for America's national security and economic interests that the alleged crime, corruption and incompetence at the USCIS be reported and rooted out. Considering Senate Majority Leader Harry Reid has tagged immigration reform "as one of the 10 most important legislative priorities for the 111th Congress," let's be candid—anything less and the problems will never be solved.

While Aytes tried to minimize the crime and corruption at the USCIS to a "few" employees, it is more extensive than I reported. A cursory search on Google will provide anyone with scores of examples. Like this one: "Atlanta, GA – Hashukh C. Patel, a Business Interface Representative for U.S. Citizenship and Immigration Services and former USCIS Adjudication Officer, and his wife … were indicted by a federal grand jury on May 13, 2008. The indictment … charges both defendants with conspiracy to encourage … aliens to come to the U.S. [illegally] for the Patels' private financial gain."[82]

Aytes contends that my article characterized the agency as "basically inhabited by crooks and thugs." Those are his words, not mine but I do concur that the agency's checkered history can paint that grim picture but no, not every federal employee is a crook or thug.

Bribery, be it for cash, gifts or for sex is but one criminal element at the USCIS. There are others like embezzlement and abuse of public trust. In the United States of America v. Catherine Ileen Spear, for instance, according to the indictment, "Catherine Spear worked as a federal immigration employee responsible for the intake of applications submitted by persons applying for changes in their immigration status. Instead of processing the applications, she kept the fees accompanying the applications and then threw the applications in the trash."[83]

I would argue that it is not my reporting that "tarnishes" the USCIS' 18,000 federal employees, as Aytes alleges, rather it is the corrupt federal officials who tarnish it coupled by the agency's record of inefficiency which includes the accumulation of a 20-year backlog of applications that contributes to an environment that invites corruption in the first place. As I previously reported, a December 2008 Homeland Security Threat assessment determined that long immigration waits encourage foreigners to enter illegally. If Aytes takes this threat assessment at face value, then the USCIS is exacerbating America's immigration problems. A private sector company with that record would have been out of business years ago. I am simply reporting a record that USCIS' top chief apparently does not want the public to know anything about.

Now let's look at an area where Aytes and I agree. Indeed, the USCIS plays a critical role in America's immigration system. As he wrote in his reprimand: "As the gatekeepers of the United States' immigration system, we all serve on the front lines of our homeland defense."

Which is why fixing the problems at USCIS is an urgent issue of national security.

Ironically Aytes bolstered my reporting, perhaps unwittingly, when he stated how the "USCIS established the Office of Security and Integrity (OSI) in 2007 ... In doing so," Aytes wrote, "we tripled the resources dedicated to this critical mission ..." because as his statement suggests the crime and corruption at the USCIS had to have reached such high levels that a new bureaucracy with resources *tripled* (italics mine) was created to try to curb it.

While I appreciate how Aytes boosted my article's thesis, I would be remiss if I did not point out something he declined to mention. Depending on who is bribing federal officials; be it someone linked to terrorism, or wanted for other crimes, such as murder or drug smuggling—other law enforcement agencies like the FBI, Terrorism Task Force or various district attorney offices' valuable resources supplement the USCIS' resources to combat the crime and corruption that originated out of USCIS.

Moreover, Aytes must know I am not the only person who has shined a light on America's immigration problems. Does he attack them?

Case in point, President Barack Obama shined a light. In fact, the Obama White House plans to "fix the dysfunctional immigration bureaucracy." Aytes took issue with me in his letter when I described the bureaucracy as "nonsensical." I guess we can debate semantics with the White House here.

Additionally Aytes was displeased when I described the bureaucracy as "degrading" which was backed up with this example. "A USCIS adjudicator was arrested after he was caught on tape, telling a 22-year old Colombian woman, 'I want sex,' he said ... 'You get your Green card.'"[84] Degrading? Yes or no? Read more troubling encounters at Aytes' "superb organization" at the *New York Times*.[85]

Then there is Senator John McCain's point of view of Aytes "superb organization." McCain "believes America's immigration system is broken." During his failed presidential bid, McCain committed to clear out the backlog where people have waited for "up to twenty years."

Another consideration is Congressman Zoe Lofgren's findings. In a July 30, 2007, for instance, Lofgren's office in a press release said, "USCIS has consistently failed to reduce application backlogs and has suffered from a lack of transparency and effective management … 'After repeated requests over several months, USCIS has yet to provide Congress with a detailed plan.'"

Even last Friday Homeland Security Secretary Janet Napolitano—on the job for a little over a week showed she is aware of the problems and issued a wide-ranging immigration directive asking in part "what progress has been made in reducing the significant backlogs" referring to those pesky backlogs that accumulated in Aytes' "superb organization" that I contend "overwhelm" the agency and created an environment for crime and corruption to occur. Frankly, this is an easy connect-the-dots situation. Were the aforementioned tarnishing USCIS' honorable reputation as well, as Aytes accused me of doing, when they criticized it or were they drawing a conclusion based on USCIS' record?

In closing, to eliminate the absurd notion that I could "tarnish" Aytes' "superb organization" recall, if you will, that it was the INS (now USCIS) who six months to the day after Mohamed Atta and Marwan Al-Shehhi slammed planes into the World Trade Center, killing 3000 people who "notified a Venice, Florida, flight school that the two men had been approved for student visas." It seems clear to me that everyone is aware of the serious problems at the USCIS except the USCIS' Michael Aytes, but everyone may not know just how serious the problems are—be it criminal or procedural.

I would like to request an interview with Aytes. I would like to report what it is like for an "Immigration Officer with more than 30 years' experience" serving in a dysfunctional (President Obama's description, not mine) bureaucracy, where year after year colleagues were indicted for bribery among other crimes and report his experience back to the public. Americans might want to know how this agency tasked in part to protect their national security was broken (Sen. McCain's description, not mine).

I accept Aytes "challenge." In doing so Aytes will discover that he mischaracterized me as "someone with very limited knowledge of the U.S. immigration system." I stand by my article. The question is will Aytes stand by his letter?

8·

TERRORISTS HAVE APPLIED FOR GREEN CARDS

NATIONAL SECURITY ALERT!
Terrorists continue to exploit broken immigration system.

• **Immigration Reform: Terrorists have applied for Green Cards**— headline, *Peschmann archives,* March 15, 2010.[86] Below is an excerpt from an article I wrote referencing the Government and Accountability Office Report: Immigration Benefits: Actions Needed to Address Vulnerabilities in Process for Granting Permanent Residency, December 2008.[87] Summary quoted after this excerpt. There is more on this breach to national security topic later in the timeline.

"Terrorists and other individuals posing a threat to national security have applied for lawful permanent residency"—the Green Card. The "available data" provided to the GAO found that the "USCIS background checks identified individuals who were (1) KSTs [Known or suspected terrorist], (2) associates of terrorists, (3) involved in providing material support to terrorists or terrorist organizations, and (4) agents of a foreign government involved in espionage. From March 2003 through December 1, 2007, FDNS [Office of Fraud Detection and National Security] received about 14,500 national security referrals for all application types. According to FDNS officials, about 10 percent involved individuals on TSC's [Terrorist Screening Center] watch list and the balance of these cases involved individuals who were not on the terrorist watch list, but whose background checks indicated other possible national security concerns, such as those having associations with known or suspected terrorists.

The same applies for the Federal Bureau of Investigations.

As the GAO report documents: "In addition to identifying potential national security concerns from checking an alien's name against watch lists in TECS [Treasury Enforcement Communications System], name checks against the FBI's investigative files have uncovered individuals who raised national security concerns. We reviewed a random sample created by FDNS of FBI name check results provided to USCIS to ascertain the types of national security concerns identified during the name check process. We found that the FBI provided information to USCIS that these individuals

• had associated with terrorist organizations,
• were agents of foreign governments,
• were involved in criminal activities, or
• had engaged in espionage against the United Sates

While USCIS has some data on applicants with national security concerns, the data are limited because USCIS's CLAIMS [Computer Linked Application Information Management System] was not designed to capture and routinely generate reports on the extent, type, and nature of national security threats posed by applicants. For example, this system does not routinely provide statistics on the visa categories used (e.g., family- or employment-based applications) and whether the immigration benefits were granted or denied. Such information could be useful to help identify the characteristics of applicants who could pose national security and terrorism-related concerns, and the avenues they may use to stay in the United States.

That said, to be fair, the GAO report noted that some action has been taken to improve the agencies performance, such as increasing staffing, but the report clearly states that the "USCIS has not completed actions necessary to address identified vulnerabilities.

NATIONAL SECURITY ALERT!

As of this writing, the GAO Report documenting the above article excerpt is the most recent and recommendations remain open. **NATIONAL SECURITY ALERT!**

As of this writing, the GAO Report documenting the above article excerpt is the most recent and recommendations remain open.

• Source: Government and Accountability Office Report: Immigration Benefits: Actions Needed to Address Vulnerabilities in Process for Granting Permanent Residency, December 2008, summary below.[88]

Since September 11, 2001, a concern has been that terrorists or their supporters would seek to immigrate to the United States (i.e., seek lawful permanent residency (LPR)). The Department of Homeland Security's U.S. Citizenship and Immigration Services (USCIS) conducts background checks and the FBI conducts name checks for those applying for LPR. GAO was asked to review USCIS's processes for screening individuals applying for LPR. GAO assessed: (1) what available data show about the extent to which national security concerns were discovered during USCIS background checks for LPR applications, (2) what issues USCIS has encountered in its background check processes and what actions have been taken to resolve those issues, and (3) the extent to which USCIS has addressed fraud vulnerabilities in its adjudication procedures for LPR. To conduct this work, GAO analyzed USCIS background check and adjudication procedures, USCIS data on adjudications, and its assessments of fraud in applications for LPR, and interviewed USCIS and FBI officials.

Available data show that of the approximately 917,000 applications for LPR USCIS received from January 1, 2006, through May 31, 2007, 516 (0.05 percent) were referred to USCIS's Office of Fraud Detection and National Security (FDNS) for national security concerns. According to FDNS, the cases referred to it involved individuals on a watch list which included names of known and suspected terrorists, or posed other national security concerns such as individuals who associated with suspected terrorists or engaged in espionage. While USCIS's application case management system was not designed to capture and routinely generate detailed statistics on those posing national security concerns, FDNS has developed a separate system to capture such data. USCIS had encountered delays in obtaining the results of FBI name checks--FBI checks of its investigative files--for LPR applicants and others, and had issues regarding the usefulness of these results, but USCIS and the FBI have taken a number of actions that have improved these checks. The FBI dedicated more staff to process name checks, and USCIS provided additional funding and training to FBI staff. As a result, the number of pending name checks has decreased 90 percent, from 329,000 in May 2007 to 32,000 as of September 30, 2008. The FBI plans on being able to complete all name checks within 90 days of receipt by June 2009. *USCIS has taken some actions to address vulnerabilities identified in one of its assessments of fraud, called Benefit Fraud and Compliance Assessments (BFCA), but has yet to complete actions to address vulnerabilities identified in four other BFCAs.* To conduct BFCAs, FDNS selected a sample of petitions to determine the extent of fraud and identify any systemic vulnerabilities in USCIS's adjudications processes. Internal control standards call for agency managers to promptly evaluate findings from audits and reviews, determine proper actions to take, and complete them within established time frames. Although FDNS completed all of these assessments between June 2006 and September 2007, *USCIS has not established time frames for evaluating these findings and implementing any necessary corrective actions. Until USCIS takes corrective actions, vulnerabilities identified by these BFCAs will persist, increasing the risk that ineligible individuals will obtain LPR status. Lack of verification of the evidence submitted with petitions is one of the major vulnerabilities identified in these BFCAs. For example, FDNS staff found that individuals claiming to be married were not, employers did not exist, and aliens did not have the education or skills they claimed. USCIS procedures give its staff discretion on deciding whether to verify evidence submitted with petitions.* The BFCAs have shown that adjudicators following these procedures have approved fraudulent petitions. Verifying all petitioner-submitted evidence is impossible. Procedures that require verifying certain evidence under certain circumstances would *help adjudicators better detect fraud and help USCIS maintain the balance between fraud detection and USCIS's customer service and production-related objectives* [italics mine].

SETTING FIRE TO MONEY ALERT!

Don't forget that when Bush left office, he authorized a second $500 million appropriation/bailout to the USCIS for their perpetual quest to modernize and reform. As you will see, it is not successful and legal immigrants still suffer right now. When politicians like the "Gang of Eight" say the system needs to be modernized the truth is the USCIS has had years to modernize and the funds to do it to no avail. Do not be deceived.

SETTING FIRE TO MONEY ALERT!

Don't forget that when Bush left office he authorized a second $500 million appropriation/bailout to the USCIS for their perpetual quest to modernize and reform. As you will see, it is not successful and legal immigrants still suffer right now. When politicians like the "Gang of Eight" say the system needs to be modernized the truth is the USCIS has had years to modernize and the funds to do it to no avail. Do not be deceived.

The Gang of Eight: Republican senators: Marco Rubio (R-FL.), Jeff Flake (R-AZ), John McCain (R-AZ), and Lindsey Graham (R-SC). Democrat senators: Dick Durbin (D-IL.), Chuck Schumer (D-NY), Michael Bennet (D-CO) and Robert Menendez (D-NJ).[89]

• **Immigration to go paperless**—headline, *Washington Post*, November 7, 2008.[90] "If successful, the five-year, $500 million effort to convert U.S. Citizenship and Immigration Services' case-management system from paper-based to electronic could reduce backlogs and processing delays by at least 20 percent, and possibly more than 50 percent, people close to the project said."

9.

LEGAL IMMIGRATION BAILOUT

NOTE: Below is an article I wrote in 2009 shining a light on the immigration crisis. It still applies today.

There is another crisis on the verge of catching fire in America and the bailout has already begun. It is the bailout to fix the costly fallout created by decades of failed immigration policies that taxpayers and lawful immigrants have been funding and will continue to fund to mop up the mess.

In November 2008, a fraction of the bailout or appropriations went to the U.S. Citizenship and Immigration Services (USCIS), a $2.6 billion-a-year agency. The USCIS received $500 million over five years to modernize its case management system. This agency, tasked with protecting America's national security while balancing the nation's economic needs and humanitarian desires, intends to modernize by transferring paper applications to electronic filings. This move by the Bush administration was a last-minute rescue because the failure to properly modernize this perilously dysfunctional bureaucracy had produced twenty-year backlogs of paperwork that cost hundreds of millions of taxpayer dollars to store in the interim.

According to the *Washington Post*: "Government investigators have reported that the [USCIS'] pre-computer-age paper filing system incurs $100 million a year in archiving, storage, retrieval and shipping costs; has led to the loss or misplacement of more than 100,000 files; and has contributed to backlogs and delays for millions of cases."[91]

According to the USCIS website, under former acting Director Jonathan Scharfen, the agency "anticipates processing times no longer than 10-12 months." "Anticipates" is the operative word because this $500 million bailout was not the first installment intended to address the backlog. According to President Bush's fiscal

2003 immigration budget, another "five-year, $500-million initiative" was granted to the Immigration Naturalization Services' (now USCIS') "comprehensive" backlog elimination plan "to achieve ... a six-month processing-time standard." Seven years and $500 million later, the problem still exists. The USCIS' inefficiency turned U.S. law and order into a travesty where following the law became a roll of the dice, and a cruel, heart-wrenching exercise in futility for countless lawful foreign nationals who sought America's dream. These backlogs grew under the Clinton and Bush administrations and contributed to the 12-20 million illegal aliens living in the "shadows." According to a December 2008 Homeland Security Department intelligence threat assessment, "Long waits for immigration ... will cause more foreigners to try to enter the U.S. illegally."

It gets worse. How does this failure affect national security? With a chaotic USCIS, who could determine who is in America legally and who should be deported? Are millions of illegal aliens wallowing for decades in the USCIS' backlog or did they not bother to file? Do they seek to harm Americans? It is impossible to know.

But the burden for the USCIS' dereliction of duty manifests in other ways: taxpayers fund government lawyers to defend its ineptitude.

Under 8 United States Code § 1447(b) lawful immigrants may file a lawsuit after a "reasonable" period of time, compelling the USCIS to act if the agency "has failed to issue a decision on a properly filed immigration application." Called a Writ of Mandamus, it does not force the USCIS to reach a favorable result, but "to take action that it is legally obligated to take."

Who defends the USCIS' inability to perform its job? The taxpayer-funded Office of Immigration litigation (OIL), part of the U.S. Department of Justice. According to Justice, OIL employs "approximately 250 attorneys" and "100 support staff." A December 2008 nationwide salary search indicates on average a trial attorney at OIL in Washington, D.C., earns $77,000 annually adding another $20 million-a-year cost burden to taxpayers. That figure does not factor in the cost of OIL's support staff or other ancillary costs to maintain this department.

Do the math. Overhauling the USCIS/INS years ago would have saved taxpayers well over $1 billion dollars on judicial interventions and storage type costs over the last decade alone.

But this ongoing immigration bailout has just begun. There are other problems to tackle such as reducing the incalculable cost of criminal illegal alien crimes against Americans. To attempt to curb this calamity (caused in large part by broken borders and a dysfunctional USCIS), last year Congress authorized another partial bailout: $200 million to fund "a fingerprint database sharing program" with $150 million more slated for the next two years. Reportedly, Congress was spurred into action after "the murder of Houston police officer Rodney Johnson ... by an illegal immigrant previously convicted of a crime, was deported," who returned to the U.S.[92]

What is needed to begin to fix immigration is the immediate restoration of law and order—plus competence at the USCIS, not lawmakers' noisy platitudes for action that invariably produce costly but minimal results.

Unfortunately, thanks to feckless lawmakers, that means more taxpayer dollars to bailout the USCIS. It is another crisis American taxpayers did not create but will fund to "fix."

[**Source:** *Peschmann archives*, January 15, 2009.][93]

10 · GAME CHANGER

NOTE: While 'experts' were predicting a landslide win for Republican presidential candidate Mitt Romney prior to the November 2012 elections, I was reporting how the election was stacked in President Obama's favor. Below is an article I wrote in September 2012 documenting why. Once you understand the system then you can see how politicians in both parties have politicized immigration by using your tax dollars to their vote-grab advantage. There is an update at the end because the same forces remain in play today and you deserve to know what's going on with your tax dollars and how it keeps politicians in power.

With the help of President George W. Bush, President Barack Obama may win re-election by taking a page out of President Bill Clinton's 1996 re-election playbook. How? By using taxpayer-funded programs that teach immigrant Green card holders how to become U.S. citizens—thereby increasing likely Democratic voters.[94]

During the Clinton era it was called Citizenship USA (CUSA).[95] Today, it's the Citizenship and Integration Grant Program that's similar to then Senator Obama's Citizenship Promotion Act of 2007, a bill he introduced with Rep. Luis Gutierrez (D-IL) to give "$80 million" in grants to community organizers "to assist" legal "aliens" in becoming U.S. citizens.[96] Obama's bill would have sped up FBI background checks. During the Clinton's CUSA program, FBI background checks were rushed or ignored so felons became U.S. citizens in time to vote. And thanks to President Bush, by executive order, promoting citizenship is the law of the land. Obama no longer requires congressional approval.

But first, let's rewind to the Clinton administration. While most people associate President Clinton's impeachment with Monica Lewinsky, Linda Tripp, and sex in the Oval Office that's not the full story.[97] Amid the impeachment inquiry, other investigations were taking place that were not included within the articles of impeachment because of time limitations.

One investigation focused on the Immigration Naturalization Services (INS), now the United States Citizenship and Immigration Services (USCIS), during the 1996 Bill Clinton vs. Bob Dole presidential contest. At issue was whether or not the Clinton White House abused its power for political gain by misusing the INS and circumventing the rule of law to increase the number of likely Democrat voters. According to David Schippers, the chief investigative counsel for the Clinton impeachment investigation, in a conversation with this journalist, the answer was "yes."

As Schippers wrote in his bestselling book, *Sell Out: The Inside Story of the President Clinton's Impeachment,* (Regnery Publishing, Inc. 2000): "The White House pressured the INS into expediting its 'Citizenship USA' (CUSA) program to grant citizenship to thousands of aliens that the White House counted as likely Democratic voters.[98] To ensure maximum impact, INS concentrated on aliens in key states—California, Florida, Illinois, New York, New Jersey, and Texas—that hold a combined 181 electoral votes, just 89 short of the total needed to win the election."

To meet the deadline to naturalize a stated goal of one million new citizens in time for them to register to vote, a shortcut was necessary to "breakdown" the typical background check timeline required during the FBI fingerprint background check process.

Among his abundant documentation, Shippers obtained an email from then Vice President Al Gore's office, following President Clinton's lead, to Doug Farbrother of the National Performance Review (NPR). NPR was tasked with removing all barriers to citizenship in major cities in four swing states. To accomplish that, NPR inserted "reinventors" as part of official INS management teams "to influence INS staff who would be less inclined to complain or voice concerns if the directives came from within." The email stated: "THE PRESIDENT IS SICK OF THIS AND WANTS ACTION. IF NOTHING MOVES TODAY WE'LL HAVE TO TAKE PRETTY DRASTIC ACTIONS."

As Schippers reported, "We developed sources inside the INS with specific knowledge of the facts who revealed that FBI arrest records that were being sent to the Chicago INS office simply were not being inserted into the aliens' files. As a result, aliens with criminal records were being granted citizenship."

Predictably, the Clinton White House, the INS, and the Justice Department denied any political motivation for speeding up the citizenship program, however, a 1996 audit of CUSA by KPMG Peat Marwick documented the fruits of their labor and found the United States got:

1. More than 75,000 new citizens who had arrest records when they applied;

2. An additional 115,000 citizens whose fingerprints were unclassifiable for various technical reasons and were never resubmitted; and

3. Another 61,000 people who were given citizenship with no fingerprints submitted at all."

Schippers, a Democrat, concluded "thousands of criminals are now citizens of the United States because it was assumed they would vote for Bill Clinton and Al Gore."

While the citizenship to-get-out-the-vote idea might have originated from Clinton's Chicago-styled 1996 re-election success, it is President Bush who gets the credit for paving the way for Obama's pro-citizenship efforts that have been taking place since he took office and could easily help him win re-election (it did).

A little background is necessary. In 2002, the Bush administration's Homeland Security Act created the USCIS's Office of Citizenship (OoC) "to promote instruction and training ... on citizenship responsibilities."[99]

Then on June 7, 2006, President Bush signed Executive Order 13404 to establish a "Task Force on New Americans" to "strengthen the efforts of the Department of Homeland Security (DHS) and Federal, State, and local agencies to help legal immigrants embrace the common core of American civic culture, learn our common language, and fully become Americans."[100]

The following federal departments were included in the order: DHS, State, Treasury, Defense, Justice, Agriculture, Commerce, Labor, Health and Human Services, Housing and Urban Development, and Education.

The New American Task Force was ordered, in part, to: "provide direction [to legal immigrants] ... concerning the integration into American society ... particularly through instruction in English, civics, and history." Funding was determined by the secretary of the DHS.

Under the Obama administration, Bush's New American task force became in part the USCIS' Citizenship and Integration Grant Program where the OoC coordinates with President Obama's Director of White House Domestic Policy Council Cecilia Muñoz.[101] Prior to serving at the White House, Muñoz worked at the National Council of La Raza, the nation's largest Latino civil rights organization.[102] Muñoz has thus far not responded to an interview request.

According to a Government Accountability Office (GAO) report: Immigrant Integration: U.S. Citizenship and Immigration Services Could Better Assess Its Grant Program, in 2010, Obama's Domestic Policy Council formed the Interagency Working Group on the Federal Role of Immigrant Integration to assess how the federal government could best "coordinate integration efforts across agencies." Obama's committee includes representatives from Janet Napolitano's Department of Homeland Security, Eric Holder's Justice Department, Arne Duncan's Education Department, Kathleen Sebelius's Health and Human Services Department, and Hilda Solis's Labor Department, *as well as several Executive Offices of the President* [italics mine]."[103]

While the scope and funding of these programs remain secret because GAO officials "were unable to meet with officials from the White House," and inquiries from this journalist have thus far gone unanswered, following is some of what we know.

Obama's Citizenship and Integration grant program was established in 2009 "pursuant to the Consolidated Security, Disaster Assistance and Continuing Appropriations Act, 2009," The program "awarded grants to organizations promoting the rights and responsibilities of citizenship."

From "2008 to 2011, OoC reported conducting more than 300 significant outreach events." Nearly half of OoC's funding—about $19.8 million—"was spent on grants aimed at preparing immigrants for the naturalization process .... Civic integration included OoC's citizenship programs; economic integration included refugee resettlement assistance provided by the Department of Health and Human Services; and linguistic integration included English language acquisition grants provided to states by the Department of Education. *The data do not represent all federal programs that support immigrant integration and do not provide a complete estimate of federal funding because a number of programs did not report a funding amount* [italics mine]."

According to the USCIS OoC, some groups that have received grants include: Access California Services, an organization that serves 'the Arab American & Muslim American Communities'; Central American Resource Center, a Latino Resource and Justice Center; various church charities; Asian groups; and the International Rescue Committee, Inc. (IRC).[104] The IRC, according to its website, lists people like Madeline Albright, Kofi Annan, Condoleezza Rice, H.R.H. Princess Firyal of Jordan, Henry Kissinger, Tom Brokaw, and Scott Pelley as "overseers."

According to the GAO report, in 2010, "Thirteen federal agencies across the federal government reported offering a total of 79 [immigrant integration] programs (self-reported). 'Some programs' served the general population but include the immigrant and non-immigrant 'populations as a subset' such as 'the Department of Agriculture's National School Lunch Program' which 'offers low-cost or free lunches to children from low-income families.'

Michelle Obama's lunch program is but one example of where these citizenship programs appear, however, one cannot report the magnitude or the taxpayer cost because yet again the Obama administration is *not* being transparent.

As a GAO footnote states: "OoC identified other agencies with programs supporting immigrant integration that *did not respond to the data request* (italics mine).

While the USCIS and the GAO provide slightly different funding numbers for the USCIS' OoC grant program, to add some context to the cost, in May 2012, one USCIS grant opportunity totaled $5 million; now extrapolate outwards.[105]

Remember, this amount is separate from the ongoing citizenship programs that span across thirteen federal agencies.

It is worth noting that like Clinton's CUSA vote-grab effort that targeted likely Democrat voters in key states–California, Florida, Illinois, New York, New Jersey, and Texas to ensure maximum electoral votes, so goes Obama's Ooc grant program.[106]

If past is prologue, expect the first community organizer president, Barack Obama's, re-election effort to wildly benefit from these taxpayer funded citizenship programs to increase likely Democratic voters. After all, promoting citizenship and naturalizing selective immigrants in a broken, backlogged immigration system just in time to vote worked for Clinton's 1996 re-election.

Problem is, both sides do this.

UPDATE: Indeed immigrant voters played a pivotal role in President Obama's 2012 re-election win with Latinos making up 10 percent of the electorate, and voting for President Obama over Mitt Romney 71 percent to 27 percent.[107]

For some perspective in 2010 1.04 million people received legal permanent resident status—139,120 of them were born in Mexico, 70,863 in China and 58,173 were born in the Philippines.[108]

Let's be blunt here. The Republican Party, after losing the White House twice to Obama, is on well-deserved self-inflicted life support. Perhaps that is because it is difficult to see the difference between the two establishment parties. The left, right paradigm is disingenuous and has morphed into a distracting soap opera.

So the cycle continues …

[**Source:** *Peschmann archives*, September 30, 2012.][109]

11·

PRESIDENT OBAMA ERA, PART I

Obama era: 2009:

INCOMPETENCE ALERT!

Obama DHS chief Janet Napolitano—on the job for a little over a week acknowledges the backlogs for legal immigrants that never go away despite the USCIS receiving 100's of millions of dollars and additional staffing to modernize. President George W. Bush hands President Barack Hussein Obama a mess.

• **Secretary Napolitano: Legal Immigration Benefit Backlogs—** *Directive,* January 30, 2009. "What progress has been made in reducing the significant backlogs that had developed in the adjudication of naturalization petitions and adjustment of status (Green Card) applications? Which regional offices still lag behind in making progress toward target processing times, and what specific steps are recommended for providing priority resources to those offices?"[110]

MIND-BENDING INCOMPETENCE ALERT!

More on why legal immigration is still Vegas-like. Despite generous funding and increased staffing, some applications are processed; others are lost or stuck in storage facilities. Incompetence begins in the mail room.

Excerpted from one of my articles: **Crime, corruption and incompetence at the USCIS Part II,**[111] quoting from **Source: Government and Accountability Office Report (GAO)**: Federal User Fees: Additional Analysis and Timely Reviews Could Improve Immigration and Naturalization User Fee Design and USCIS

Operations, January 23, 2009 (GAO summary is listed in 2007 when user fees jumped 86%).[112]

Let's start at the beginning where lawful immigrants typically first encounter the USCIS by mailing in their application with the expectation that it will be processed only to discover mailing it in does not mean it will be processed. Why not? Because at the USCIS, the basic task of counting, opening and processing the mail is unpredictable.

According to a U.S. Government Accountability Office report entitled Federal User Fees: Additional Analysis and Timely Reviews Could Improve Immigration and Naturalization User Fee Design and USCIS Operations, "Contractors perform all operations for incoming and outgoing mail at the [USCIS] service centers, and they are paid according to a fixed unit price for each piece of mail processed… and the USCIS has not developed an agency wide standard operating procedure for validating the contractors' count. As a result, three of four service centers do not validate contractor mail count at all… In most cases, however, USCIS cannot verify that it is receiving the services that it is paying for."

Why isn't there a structure in place to ensure that all applications are counted and properly processed?

The GAO report explains why. "According to USCIS Service Center Operations officials at headquarters, service centers are responsible for developing methods to validate contractor mail counts. The Vermont Service Center's "Incoming Mail Count Instruction" document and the Nebraska Service Center's standard operating procedure for incoming mail do not require USCIS employees to validate the contractors' incoming mail counts. California Service Center employees told us that they do not validate 100 percent of the incoming mail counts because a manual counting process would be inefficient and disruptive. They also said that certain types of electronic count verification such as counting the number of forms that are data entered into USCIS' data systems would be unreliable because a single piece of mail may include multiple forms. Also, mail that does not include forms would not be data entered and therefore not captured by this type of verification."

The GAO report continues: "The Texas Service Center is the exception, having developed a method for validating the contractor's mail count. USCIS employees randomly select samples of "tubs" of incoming mail multiple times each week, count the pieces of mail contained in the tubs and compare their counts to the contractor's counts for these tubs. Texas Service Center officials told us that over the course of the month, service center employees ensure that they review an adequate sample size, aggregate the difference between their sample counts and the contractor's sample counts, multiply this difference by a factor that accounts for the ratio between the sample size and the total amount of incoming mail, and apply the result to adjust the contractor's monthly total count for all incoming mail. GAO has previously reported that a basic tenet of government procurement is that before payment is made, the purchasing agency must verify that the services have been received in accordance with contractual requirements, and the price charged is proper and correct. Without doing so, USCIS may be paying its contractors for services that it has not received."

The unprocessed applications according to the GAO report, "at the Texas Service Center… were stored outside in six rented 10-by-40-foot containers, double-locked, and monitored by a full-time security guard." Welcome to step one of legal immigration.

CRIME & CORRUPTION ALERT!

• **Roy Bailey a former top immigration official in Detroit whose "outrageous conduct" involved taking free meals, landscaping services and casino chips in return for official favors**—*U.S. District court eastern district of Michigan Southern Division indictment.* March 9, 2009. Case No. 07-CR-20327-01 Bailey… pled guilty "to defrauding the federal government, conspiracy to commit bribery, and failing to report a felony…." "Under Roy Bailey's control, the immigration system… was starkly divided between those he favored and those he did not."[113]

• **The Mexicanization of American law enforcement**—headline, *City Journal,* Autumn 2009. "Corruption indictments and convictions linked to drug-trafficking organizations, known in police parlance as DTOs, are popping up in FBI press releases with disturbing frequency. In April, for instance, the U.S. Attorney's office in the

Southern District of Texas announced that Sergio Lopez Hernandez, a 40-year-old Customs and Border Protection inspector, had been convicted of drug trafficking, alien smuggling, and bribery. Hernandez pleaded guilty to accepting over $150,000 in bribes and to conspiring to sell cocaine and bring illegal aliens into the country." "Last year, FBI officials tell [Judith Miller], the Bureau worked on nearly 2,500 public corruption cases and convicted more than 700 dishonest public servants throughout the nation. Most of them were unrelated to the cartels, and Special Agent Abbott, of the FBI's criminal branch in El Paso, says that only 15 to 30 of his region's cases so far have involved drug-related corruption among law enforcement officials. "But given the damage that can be done by just one corrupt officer or inspector," he adds, "this is an important vulnerability. We know it."[114]

• **Jeweler, former diplomat plead guilty to exchanging visas for jewelry, trips with dancers**—headline, *Associated Press,* February 25, 2009. Mike O'Keefe was the deputy nonimmigrant visa chief at the U.S. consulate. O'Keefe personally fast-tracked visa applications for New York-based STS Jewels. In exchange, he received the presents from Sunil Agrawal, the chief executive officer of STS Jewels, according to court documents.[115]

• **Corruption in immigration agency endangers Americans**—headline, *Detroit News/Family Security Matters,* March 11, 2009. "Talal Chahine is indeed a fugitive. He was the person who arranged the marriage fraud than enabled a woman by the name of Nada Nadim Prouty to acquire resident alien status by engaging in a marriage fraud after her 1988-issued student visa to the United States expired. Having acquired lawful immigrant status as a result of that marriage fraud, she ultimately became a United States citizen and then went on to secure a job with the FBI as a special agent! She had a gun, a badge and a security clearance that she apparently put to good use, accessing databases on informants and investigations into Hezbollah, a pernicious terrorist organization. She similarly accessed databases at the CIA when she left the FBI for a job with the CIA."[116]

• **Green Cards, belief and betrayal at a storefront church**—headline, *New York Times,* June 16, 2009. "Word of the deal spread swiftly among Ecuadorean immigrants, along a robust grapevine from New York City... all they had to do was to fill out a form and provide $8,000 each in cash and some personal identification documents... The green cards would be ready in a month."[117]

• **Ex-judge accused of filing false immigration forms, bilking clients**—headline, *New York Law Journal,* July 15, 2009. "Former Manhattan Civil Court Judge Salvador Collazo was arrested early Tuesday morning by federal authorities for a conspiracy to commit visa fraud and overcharge clients."[118]

• **FBI says corrupt border officials accepting bribes expose U.S. to terrorist risk**—headline, *ABC News.* September 24, 2009. "At the U.S.-Mexico border, FBI video surveillance... caught a truck full of illegal immigrants pulling up to Customs and Border Protection officer Michael Gilliland, and being waved through his border inspection lane for $100,000, officials said... in Texas, an undercover FBI operation allegedly caught a deputy sheriff in the act. "You can either pay me here or follow me all the way to Petula and you can pay the judge," the deputy sheriff told an undercover FBI agent posing as a Mexican national."[119]

USCIS ATTACKS TRUTH TELLERS ALERT!

In 2009 USCIS Acting Deputy Director Michael Aytes (a 30-year bureaucrat) tries to attack my credibility for daring to report the crime, corruption and incompetence at the USCIS and fails. The corruption is so bad, the USCIS has **tripled** the budget to try and combat it. He has declined my interview request.

• Former USCIS Acting Deputy Director Michael Aytes in a letter directed at me stated: "the **USCIS established the Office of Security and Integrity (OSI) in 2007" to deal with the problem of crime and corruption at USCIS, "We tripled the resources dedicated to this critical mission."[120]** The OSI tripled the resources ostensibly because of the escalating as opposed to the diminishing ongoing corruption at this agency. See *Chapter 7: USCIS Attacks* or the appendix for his letter in its entirety.

NATIONAL SECURITY ALERT!

More on the Radical Islamic Jihadi threat and how they exploit America's broken immigration system. Marriage fraud seen in the 1980's remains an issue.

• **Radical Islamic terrorists and America's immigration crisis**
Below is an excerpt from an article I wrote reporting from a *2009 Virginia Terrorism Threat Assessment,* March 2009 (Law Enforcement Sensitive).[121]

Among the groups in America are members of; Al-Qa'ida, Al-Shabaab, HAMAS, Hizballah, Jama'at al-Tabligh, Jama'at ul Fuqra, Lashkar-e Tayyiba, the Muslim Brotherhood, Sunni Extremists, Palestinian Islamic Jihad, Islamic Jihad Union, and the Taliban.

Marriage fraud is a common method of facilitating the extended stays of foreign terrorists in the U.S. Known cases of sham marriages exist involving al-Qa'ida, Hizballah, and individuals with radical ties. Fraudulent marriages have enabled individuals affiliated with al-Qa'ida, Hizballah, and the Palestinian Islamic Jihad to remain in the U.S. One regional example is the Charlotte Hizballah cell, where a key figure "helped secure three fraudulent visas and three sham marriages for the purpose of 'legally' bringing in the United States his brother, his brother-in-law, and sister so that they might become legal permanent residents... one Virginia-linked case occurred in which a Norfolk police officer testified against an Ohio-based Jordanian man who had tried to recruit him online for a terrorist cause. Subsequent federal investigation showed this subject likely entered the U.S. through a fraudulent marriage to a Kansas City woman in 2001; the marriage was annulled five months later ... Many individuals enter the U.S. on student visas and never enroll in school... [or] individuals may enroll and seem to be legitimate students but may still be working as operatives. The three categories of nonimmigrant student visas monitored and tracked by DHS are F visas for academic study, M visas for vocational study, and J visas for cultural exchange. Such visas can be exploited by terrorists not only as a method to legally penetrate the borders, but also present a legitimate opportunity to study technical fields which may be of use in future attacks.

One of the FBI's most wanted subjects, Aafia Siddiqui, who has ties to al-Qa'ida, entered the U.S. on a student visa and lived in the country for over a decade while studying and teaching at Brandeis and MIT... she was found with handwritten notes referring to a 'mass casualty attack' at various prominent locations in the U.S., such as the Empire State Building, Statue of Liberty, Wall Street, and the Brooklyn Bridge... Separate FBI reporting advised that an individual in the U.S. had sponsored several individuals from Egypt to enter to the U.S. on F-1 student visas. This individual had an identified contact at Strayer University who prepared and filed the visa paperwork through the University... The sponsor and the university contact allegedly hold radical Muslim beliefs.

KILLING THE AMERICAN DREAM ALERT!

The American dream dies for countless skilled legal immigrants.

- **Source: Immigration attorney Carl Shusterman**

"On April 8, the State Department published the May 2009 Visa Bulletin online. Gone is the much-lamented six-year wait for green cards for professionals and skilled workers who are being sponsored by their employers. Instead, green cards are "unavailable" in this category for the next 5 months. This is the earliest that the category has become unavailable in my 33 years of practicing immigration law. Persons who have played by the rules and have pending applications for adjustment of status now have no idea when, or even if, they will qualify for permanent residence in the U.S. They live in fear of their temporary visas expiring, their children "aging out" and losing their jobs before they can secure green cards. U.S. employers are fit to be tied. At considerable expense, they obtained temporary working visas for employees filling important positions in their companies. They unsuccessfully attempted to recruit U.S. workers for job vacancies, and obtained approved PERM applications and immigrant visa petitions...Hospitals in rural and inner city locations are particularly hard hit. It is impossible to obtain temporary visas for RNs despite the growing national shortage...It is folly to think that we can guarantee healthcare coverage to all Americans as long as hundreds of thousands of nursing jobs remain vacant.... Immigrants who followed the complex immigration rules will get the following message: Never mind that you paid your taxes and never got so much as a parking ticket, that you were active in your church and that your children were straight A students, that you always maintained your legal status in the U.S. For you, the American Dream is over."[122]

Obama era: 2010

CRIME & CORRUPTION ALERT!

• **Feds: Calif. man ran student visa fraud ring**—headline, *Associated Press,* March 9, 2010. A California man was charged Monday with operating a ring of illegal test-takers who helped dozens of Middle Eastern nationals obtain U.S. student visas by passing various proficiency and college-placement exams for them, federal authorities said.[123]

• **Immigration agency attorney convicted of Federal corruption charges for taking thousands of dollars in bribes from immigrants seeking status in U.S.**—headline, *U.S. Department of Justice,* April 2010. Los Angeles – A senior attorney with U.S. Immigration and Customs Enforcement (ICE) was found guilty today of three dozen corruption-related charges for taking a series of bribes from immigrants who were seeking documentation to remain in the United States. ICE Assistant Chief Counsel Constantine Peter Kallas, 39, of Alta Loma, was convicted by a federal jury... The jury found Kallas guilty of conspiracy, six counts of bribery, two counts of obstruction of justice, seven counts of fraud and misuse of entry documents, three counts of aggravated identity theft, nine counts of making false statements to the Department of Labor, four counts of making false statements to obtain federal employee compensation, and four counts of tax evasion. "Mr. Kallas was a corrupt government official who abused his position of trust to line his own pockets," said United States Attorney André Birotte Jr."[124]

• **GAO sting shows passport fraud remains a problem**—headline, *nextgov,* July 30, 2010. "Despite multiple indicators of fraud and identity theft in each application, State identified only two as fraudulent during its adjudication process, and mailed five genuine

U.S. passports to undercover GAO mailboxes, Gregory Kutz, GAO's managing director of forensic audits and investigations told members of a Senate Judiciary Committee panel Thursday. U.S. passports are one of the most sought-after travel documents in the world, Kutz noted, because they allow holders entrance to the United States and visa-free passage to many other countries. As such, passport fraud is a serious threat to national security, he said."[125]

• **Feds issue terror watch for the Texas/Mexico border—** headline, *Fox News,* May 26, 2010. "The Department of Homeland Security is alerting Texas authorities to be on the lookout for a suspected member of the Somalia-based Al Shabaab terrorist group who might be attempting to travel to the U.S. through Mexico, a security expert who has seen the memo tells *FOXNews.com.* The warning follows an indictment unsealed this month in Texas federal court that accuses a Somali man in Texas of running a "large-scale smuggling enterprise" responsible for bringing hundreds of Somalis from Brazil through South America and eventually across the Mexican border. Many of the illegal immigrants, who court records say were given fake IDs, are alleged to have ties to other now-defunct Somalian terror organizations that have merged with active organizations like Al Shabaab, al-Barakat and Al-Ittihad Al-Islami."[126]

FUN FACT FOR LEGAL IMMIGRANTS!

Legal immigration requires several steps. There are many categories as well. The Fee Schedule is currently nine pages long. If you decide not to go to the USCIS website and see it in its entirety below is a taste I have recreated for you.

Legal immigration user fees schedule. **Source:** USCIS website.[127]

Form Title #	Title	USCIS Fees
I-129S	Nonimmigrant Petition Based on Blanket L Petition	Some petitioners must pay a **$500** Fraud Prevention and Detection Fee. If a petitioner must pay the $500 fee, they may also be subject to pay **$2,250** filing fee, mandated by Public Law 111-230
I-I30	Petition for Alien Relative	**$420**

I-485	Application to Register Permanent Residence or Adjust Status	**$985** NOTE: Does not include different subcategories where different fees apply. Such as the fee for Form I-485 Supplement A is $1,000 in addition to the fee required with your Form I-485. If you have filed Form I-485 separately, attach a copy of your filing receipt and pay only the additional fee of $1,000.
I-526	Immigrant Petition by Alien Entrepreneur	**$1,500**
I-602	If filing with form I-821 for Initial Registration and requesting EAD, And older than 14 and younger than 66.	**$380**
I-140	Immigrant Petition for Alien Worker	**$580**

INCOMPETENCE ALERT!

The USCIS also periodically changes forms. A legal immigrant can be knocked out of line for having an old form while sitting in a backlog for years and not knowing about the change of forms until it is too late. *Who knew legal immigrants are supposed to be clairvoyant!* Meanwhile the USCIS still cannot get it together.

• **Source: Government and Accountability Office Report:** Fee Design Characteristics and Trade-Offs Illustrated by USCIS's Immigration and Naturalization Fees, Mar 23, 2010, excerpt of summary below.[128]

In 2007, USCIS completed a fee review to determine the level at which fees should be set to recover the full cost of its services and increased application fees by an average of 86 percent. USCIS is preparing its first fee review since the 2007 fee increase. It is critical that USCIS and the Congress have the best possible information when overseeing these fees and the operations they fund. This testimony focuses on (1) user fee design and implementation characteristics and criteria, (2) cost assignment and trade-offs identified in USCIS's 2007 fee review, and (3) additional considerations for fee-funded agencies. It is based on past GAO reports, which included recommendations to the Secretary of

Homeland Security (DHS). DHS agreed to consider these recommendations in their next fee review.

There are four key design and implementation characteristics of user fees--how fees are set, collected, used, and reviewed. Each design and implementation characteristics presents its own set of decisions to consider and embodies trade-offs among *the four criteria that are often used to assess user fees: equity, efficiency, revenue adequacy, and administrative burden. Equity: Equity means that everyone pays his/her fair share, but there is more than one way to think about fair share. Under the beneficiary-pays principle, the beneficiaries of a service pay for the cost of providing the service from which they benefit. Under the ability-to-pay principle, those who are more capable of bearing the burden of fees should pay more for the service than those with less ability to pay.* Efficiency: By requiring identifiable beneficiaries to pay for the costs of services, user fees can simultaneously constrain demand and reveal the value that beneficiaries place on the service. If those benefiting from a service do not bear the full social cost of the service, they may seek to have the government provide more of the service than is economically efficient. Revenue adequacy: Revenue adequacy is the extent to which the fee collections cover the intended share of costs. It encompasses the extent to which collections may change over time relative to the cost of the program and the concept of revenue stability, or the degree to which short-term fluctuations in economic activity and other factors affect the level of fee collections. Administrative burden: This is the cost of administering the fee, including the cost of collection and enforcement, as well as the compliance burden. Setting the fee is perhaps is the most challenging of the fee design decisions because determining the cost of the service is often quite complex and requires considering a range of issues. *One of the biggest issues in fee setting is how to define and apply the equity criterion, such as determining the overlap between beneficiaries and users, whether to employ a beneficiary pays or ability to pay equity principle, how to address fee exemptions and waivers, and finally, how to assign costs among users.* Many of these design choices described in USCIS's 2007 fee review provide transparent analysis and identify deliberate trade-offs. *However, USCIS did not conduct the analysis necessary to fully inform either congressional decision making or USCIS's internal deliberations on key areas such as the cost of activities funded by statutorily-set fees that led to unknown cross-subsidizations.* When fees are supposed to cover all or a set portion of the costs of an agency or activity the criterion of "revenue adequacy" may be especially important to consider. For example, a reserve is important for fully fee-funded programs because it provides a cushion if program costs would not drop proportionally with a drop in fee collections. A reserve could also help support preparation for any anticipated surge in users, especially if fee collections would come after the expenditures to prepare for the surge [italics mine].

FUN FACT!

When applying for U.S. citizenship, legal immigrants/Green Card holders cannot become U.S. citizens if they answer yes to:

1. Have you **ever** been a member of in any way associated (either directly or indirectly) with:

a. The Communist Party?

b. Any other totalitarian party?

c. A terrorist organization.

2. Have you **ever** advocated *(either directly or indirectly)* the overthrow of any government by force or violence?

3. Have you **ever** persecuted *(either directly or indirectly)* any person because of race, religion, national origin, membership in a particular social group or political opinion?

4. Between March 23, 1933, and May 8, 1945, did you work for or associate in any way *(either directly or indirectly)* with:

a. The Nazi government of Germany?

b. Any government in any area (1) occupied by, (2) allied with, or (3) established with the help of the Nazi government of Germany?

c. Any German, Nazi, or S.S. military unit, paramilitary unit, self-defense unit, vigilante unit, citizen unit, police unit, government agency or office, extermination camp, concentration camp, prisoner of war camp, prison, labor camp or transit camp?

[**Source:** N-400 Application for Naturalization, DHS/USCIS, part 10, p. 7.][129]

At least that is how it used to be.

12·

FOLLY OF THE GREEN CARD-FOR INVESTOR IDEA

New York City Mayor Michael Bloomberg might want to retool some of his immigration reform initiatives within his new national coalition, the Partnership for a New American Economy, and team up with Arizona Governor Jan Brewer to tell the federal government to "do their job."[130]

Why?

Because the mayor's idea to give immigrant investors Green cards to create jobs for Americans already exists. It's called the EB-5 category for Immigrant Investors. In fact, the EB-5 has been on the books since 1990—that's over twenty years it has been the law of the land. The problem is the USCIS' inability to competently process applications.

It was last week [June 2010] when Mayor Bloomberg announced on *Fox News* an idea he had shared with the Obama administration, "You say to immigrants who have money, and are entrepreneurs from around the world, 'Come to America. We will give you a Green card. If you start a business here and employ ten or more Americans, and as long as they are still working—you keep your Green card.' It matches our needs with their needs and everyone benefits."[131]

Newsflash: according to the USCIS:

"The fifth employment-based visa preference [EB-5 Immigrant Investor Category], created by Congress in 1990, is available to immigrants seeking to enter the United States in order to invest in a new commercial enterprise that will benefit the U.S. economy and create at least 10 full-time jobs .... Acquiring lawful permanent residence ("Green card") through the EB-5 category is a three step self-petitioning process."

Too bad Mayor Bloomberg's great idea is already on the books.

So what's the problem for immigrant investors trying to create American jobs? Borrowing from James Carville, it's the government-run immigration agency, the USCIS, stupid.

Take a look. According to the Office of the Citizenship and Immigration Services Ombudsman (CIS) 2009 Annual Report to Congress:[132]

"Congress allocated approximately 10,000 immigrant visas per year to this category to make the program an important job creating engine for the United States. However, EB-5 usage rarely has exceeded 1,000 per year. EB-5 underutilization is caused by a confluence of factors, including program instability."

This is extraordinarily incompetent considering, as Senator John McCain noted during his failed 2008 presidential bid, that legal immigrants can be stuck in grueling backlogs for "twenty years," waiting to find out whether or not they have been approved to live in America. It takes a mindboggling level of ineptness for this $2.6 billion agency, the USCIS, to repeatedly fail to fill this precious job-creating quota because they cannot process applications competently.

But there is more Mayor Bloomberg and his highly respected coalition members comprised of top CEOs and mayors should know about. From page 55 of the 119-page 2009 CIS report:

Recommendation (to improve EB-5)

"1: Finalize regulations to implement the special 2002 EB-5 legislation offering certain EB-5 investors a pathway to cure deficiencies in their previously submitted petitions. The Ombudsman understands that proposed regulations have been drafted, but have been stalled in USCIS' internal rulemaking review process. As these regulations have been in the drafting and review process for over six years, they are long overdue."

And then there is this from page 12:

"USCIS document production and mailing processes have raised concerns, as there is no mechanism by which to track delivery of USCIS documents to ensure receipt by the proper recipient. Last year, the Ombudsman highlighted some of the issues that may arise from delivery problems, including lost or stolen documents and unnecessary delays."

Welcome to legal immigration in America. It's a nifty sound bite, but for countless lawful immigrants who sought America's dream—legally, it has been a cruel nightmare or an exercise in futility.

Moreover, the system becomes more anti-legal immigration by the day. For those who were able to obtain status, now the agency is taking it away and kicking out lawful business-owner immigrants, like this British couple who started a restaurant in America in 2000.

As the *New York Times* reported: "Dean and Laura Franks, a British couple who opened the restaurant in 2000, found that after nine years of running their business, they could not renew their visa, forcing them to shutter the restaurant and leave the country. [133]

The Franks are among thousands of people who enter the United States each year on E-2 visas, which allow citizens from countries with which the United States has certain trade treaties to invest in businesses and work here. The visas generally are renewed every two years, but there is no limit on how many times they can be renewed. Still, they are not intended as a path to permanent residency or citizenship.

But now, immigration advocates say they are hearing more and more accounts of renewal applications being turned down. It has been an enigmatic process for the Franks, uprooting their lives even though they have paid all their taxes, own the restaurant and its adjacent rental house, and have no debts except a mortgage on their home in Arundel, about 35 miles away.

"This is the forgotten story of immigration," said Angelo Paparelli, a prominent immigration lawyer in California. "The headlines deal with Arizona and border crossings, but these are real people too. This is what happens when you play by the rules."

In denying the Franks' renewal application last year, immigration officials said their restaurant had become a marginal business. The government sets no specific dollar amount, but it defines a marginal enterprise as one that "does not have the present or future capacity to generate more than enough income to provide a minimal living" for the visa holder and his family.

The Franks were surprised and confused to learn last year that they were deemed marginal. Their tax returns show that their gross annual income in 2008 was $64,000, in addition to rental income of $16,800. Their gross profit for the year was $38,800, which was down from their gross profit in 2007 of $50,700 because of the recession, which hit most businesses."

Clearly Mayor Bloomberg, a successful billionaire businessman, would have to agree that a private company with the problems of the USCIS would have been out of business years ago.

Meanwhile, should amnesty or some type of citizenship path become law, the USCIS is the agency tasked to process 12-20 million illegal aliens (the 2010 estimate). That's another one of Mayor Bloomberg's immigration reform initiatives and so-called solutions.

The dirty secret Washington politicians don't want people to know is how the immigration crisis, a federal-government-made disaster, occurred under both Republican and Democrat leadership when they abdicated their obligation to secure the borders and run a competent immigration agency. Mayor Bloomberg's idea for investor immigrants was a good idea. It is too bad the USCIS has failed to implement it competently for over twenty years.

[**Source:** *Peschmann archives 2010*: Immigration Reform: Mayor Bloomberg's Green-Card-for-investors idea is already law][134]

Immigration Reform: Mayor Michael Bloomberg declines to discuss his solution—that is already law, September 27, 2010.[135]

New York City Mayor Michael Bloomberg loves the press when journalists fawn over him, but dare to call him on his truthfulness and candor and he hides.

Last June 2010, Mayor Bloomberg created a media splash when he launched the Partnership for a New American Economy, a national coalition to reform immigration, where he spoke about one of his solutions—to give investors Green cards to create jobs for

Americans. But as I previously reported, the mayor's idea is not new—it's already the law. Called the EB-5 category, it's been on the books since 1990. The EB-5 provision has the virtue of being in the public domain and is easily searchable.

The problem is America's immigration agency, the United States Citizenship and Immigration Services, is incompetent and cannot process EB-5 applications properly.

I contacted Mayor Bloomberg's office to request an interview to discuss this fact. The mayor's spokesman, Jason Post, emailed me back: "We respectfully decline the opportunity."

First, I must confess, I was embarrassed for Mayor Bloomberg during his immigration reform launch that ignited speculation he would run for president because he was promoting his idea as though it were a brilliant solution when it already exists and is a failure because of a government agency. I incorrectly assumed the mayor wasn't aware of the EB-5 category.

According to Mr. Post when I initially contacted the mayor's office, this was the response I received: "We are aware of the existing EB-5 category. The mayor's proposal is different from what already exists."

Really? Then it is reasonable to ask in what way is the mayor's proposal different. It is also reasonable to ask why he didn't tell the public about the differences in the first place—but Mayor Bloomberg isn't going to answer my questions.

I also asked Bloomberg's office this: considering the fact that the USCIS cannot process the existing immigrant investor category very well, why does he think that USCIS will be able to implement his version? I cited the CIS 2009 & 2010 reports which verifies this disturbing fact.[136]

Finally, because Mayor Bloomberg advocates a path to citizenship, I also asked: Why does the Mayor think that USCIS can process millions of illegals when it cannot process legal immigrants very well? Alas, still no response.

Incidentally, during the mayor's immigration reform media blitz, he also said that somebody needs to "lead." I agree, but first, someone needs to tell the truth about the problems at the USCIS.

Sometimes it seems that politicians and lawmakers simply refuse to see things as they are or refuse to tell their constituents how things really are.

Immigration should not be about scoring political points. It is a critical issue that affects national security and the economy.

But Americans are waking up. The flame has been lit on the immigration crisis. The question is whether or not Mayor Bloomberg and Washington lawmakers will come clean and not make the immigration crisis that was created in Washington even worse.[137]

NOTE: Following is Mayor Bloomberg's line-up of co-chairs of top business leaders and politicians as part of his A Partnership for a New American Economy: Mark Hurd, former Chairman, CEO, and President of Hewlett-Packard; Robert Iger, President and CEO, Walt Disney Co.; J.W. Marriott, Jr., Chairman and CEO of Marriott International, Inc.; Jim McNerney, Chairman, President, and CEO of Boeing; Rupert Murdoch, Chairman, CEO, and Founder of News Corporation; Mayor Julián Castro of San Antonio; Mayor Phil Gordon of Phoenix; Mayor Michael Nutter of Philadelphia; and Mayor Antonio Villaraigosa of Los Angeles. Since then other notables have endorsed the idea including President Bill Clinton and Arnold Schwarzenegger. Do they know Mayor Bloomberg's bright idea is already the law?

UPDATE 2012 INCOMPETENCE ALERT!
The USCIS still cannot process the EB-5 visas competently. Precious visas continue to go unused because of the agency's perpetual ineptitude.

• **Source: 2012 CIS Ombudsman's Annual Report to Congress**, page 18. 2012[138]

• **EB-5 Immigrant Investor Program.** In 1990, Congress established the fifth employment-based (EB-5) preference category for immigrants seeking to enter the United States to engage in a commercial enterprise that will benefit the U.S. economy and directly create at least ten full- time jobs. The minimum qualifying investment amount is $500,000 for commercial enterprises located within a rural area (or targeted employment area), and is otherwise $1,000,000. This investment-based immigration category attracts individuals to the United States to supply venture capital, create jobs for U.S. workers, and stimulate the U.S. economy.

In March 2009, the Ombudsman's Office made recommendations to USCIS regarding improvements to the EB-5 program. At that time, the Ombudsman's Office reported that many of the 10,000 available EB-5 visas remained unused due to "a confluence of factors, including *program instability,* the changing economic environment, and more inviting immigrant investor programs offered by other countries." Throughout 2012, USCIS conducted extensive public engagement regarding the EB-5 program. Although the program has increased in popularity, stakeholders continue to note that **many of the same challenges encountered in 2009 continue today**. *Stakeholders also report receiving RFEs seeking information that is not related to the individual investor, but attempting to revisit issues settled during the adjudication of associated regional center applications. In addition, stakeholders also report delays in adjudication and increased processing times.* The Ombudsman's Office continues to monitor USCIS progress concerning the EB-5 program, and stakeholders are encouraged to contact the Ombudsman's Office with case specific challenges as well as suggestions for future recommendations to improve the EB-5 program [italics mine].

Access all CIS Ombudsman's Report online:[139]

MEDIA SPIN ALERT!

The article below praises the USCIS for processing about 60% of available visas. Poof! That means about 4,000 available visas have disappeared into thin air. Considering the USCIS was mandated by law to fill 10,000 visas every year since 1990 and have not fulfilled that mandate once, the USCIS has serious, mind-bending problems. What a nightmare for legal immigrants who wanted to open businesses in the USA, live freely and create jobs.

• **Record number of immigrants expected to receive EB-5 investor visas this year**—headline, *Huffington Post.* June 11, 2012. "The U.S. government is expected to issue a record 6,000-plus EB-5 immigrant investor visas to foreigners this year, *CNNMoney* reports. If the projection holds true, the government will issue nearly double the number of immigrant investor visas that they handed out last year."[140]

EB-5 ONGOING BOONDOGGLE ALERT!

Is it possible? Has the USCIS made the EB-5 investor/job creation visa program process even worse than usual? Not only is the USCIS an anti-legal immigration agency, it is an anti-job agency according to the lawsuit below. Remember the really, really smart politicians in the interest of "fairness" and "compassion," want to give citizenship to illegal aliens instead of law-abiding legal immigrants who create jobs and have to fight in court the big-government fiasco called the USCIS.

• **18 immigrants sue U.S. over entry program denials**—headline, *Associated Press,* September 18, 2012. "LOS ANGELES—Eighteen immigrants have sued the federal government to allege they were wrongly denied entry into a program that grants legal residency to foreign entrepreneurs … In a lawsuit filed Thursday in U.S. District Court in Los Angeles, the plaintiffs said they invested in a nearly $12 million project to renovate a Riverside, Calif., office building that had been vacant for two years before renting it to a tenant who created 278 jobs. The plaintiffs hail from China, India, Iran and other countries. "At a time of high unemployment, when these investments are supposed to create jobs for U.S. workers, it's difficult to understand why (U.S. Citizenship and Immigration Services) would deny the petitions of people who have put up all this money.""[141]

• **American Life sues USCIS over alleged EB-5 adjudication changes**—headline, *PRWeb,* October 9, 2012. "A lawsuit filed in September against the United States Citizenship and Immigration Services (USCIS) alleges that the federal immigration agency is missing the opportunity to create tens of thousands of American jobs and infuse hundreds of millions of investment dollars into the struggling U.S. economy by critically mismanaging the EB-5 Immigrant Investor Visa Program. The EB-5 Visa Program affords foreign citizens the opportunity to earn green cards if they invest $500,000 or $1 million in a U.S. business project that leads to the creation of 10 fulltime jobs for American workers.

The program has experienced a recent increase in popularity with both American businesses in need of financing and with foreign investors. For the 2012 fiscal year, the program had been on pace to create over 42,000 U.S. jobs and spur over $2.1 billion in U.S. investment, all at no cost whatsoever to taxpayers.

But now American Life, Inc.—one of the oldest and most successful participants in the EB-5 program— alleges in a recent lawsuit that the program's huge job creating potential is in jeopardy because the USCIS is now contradicting its previous approvals, is ignoring applicable regulations, and is dragging its feet in the regulatory process.

According to court documentation, the lawsuit, case number CV12-7893, filed in the U.S. District Court for the Central District of California on September 13th, alleges that the USCIS inconsistently denied EB-5 visas to investors in a Riverside, CA renovation project because it invalidated the methodologies used to demonstrate that the project met job creation requirements.

These applications were denied, alleges the lawsuit, even though American Life had successfully completed the same types of EB-5 projects that relied on similar job creation methodologies for over 15 years.

"The decisions by USCIS run counter to normal business practices, are irrational, arbitrary and capricious, would prevent businesses from operating in a rational manner to protect their financial interests, deprive plaintiffs of due process, and would subvert [...] foreign investors to place their funds in the United States to create jobs for qualifying American workers," states the complaint.

These changes in USCIS adjudication have now put a halt on other major EB-5 projects across the nation, such as the case with a Marriot Hotel project in Los Angeles that is already in construction phase and which could create nearly 3,400 American jobs and infuse $172 million into a suffering economy, according to the complaint."[142]

13·

PRESIDENT OBAMA ERA, PART II

Obama era: 2010 Continued

ILLEGAL ALIEN ALERT!

While lawful immigrants remain stuck, suffering in backlogs for years hoping that their applications will be processed properly, President Obama's Kenyan illegal alien Aunt Zeituni Onyango is granted asylum. Who cares that she ignored a deportation order and lived illegally in the U.S. since 2000 on government assistance? See what a big mess the USCIS is? Even President Obama's aunt with all of her nephew's mighty influence and connections could not help her get processed properly. (Did he even try to help? Who cares? Whatever.) Thanks to the media attention Aunt Zeituni gets to officially call USA home. Hooray! No equal justice in America.

• **Obama's Aunt Zeituni Onyango granted asylum**—headline, *CBS News,* May 17, 2010.[143]

GET OUT THE VOTE ALERT!

Taking a page out of President Clinton's CUSA (Citizenship USA) and President Bush's New American Task Force Executive Order playbook to integrate immigrant (Green-Card holders) to become citizens with the right to vote, see how Obama's Citizenship and Integration Grant Program is using your tax dollars.

• **USCIS announces citizenship and integration grant opportunities: funding will expand local capacity to prepare legal residents for citizenship**—headline, *USCIS Press Release.* February 2010. "WASHINGTON—U.S. Citizenship and Immigration Services (USCIS) announced today the availability of two different grants totaling $7 million designed to promote citizenship education and immigrant integration in communities across the country.

"Each aspiring citizen represents a personal story of sacrifice and triumph," said USCIS Director Alejandro Mayorkas. "This funding will increase opportunities for English language instruction, promote the rights and responsibilities that define our nation, and provide much-needed support for individuals on the path to citizenship."

The first grant will strengthen locally-based citizenship preparation programs. The second grant will increase the capacity of members or affiliates of national, regional, or statewide organizations to offer citizenship services in underserved communities. USCIS expects to announce an estimated 50 award recipients in September 2010.[144]

• **USCIS announces 2010 grant recipients and new citizenship resource center on constitution day and citizenship day**— headline, *USCIS Press Release.* September 17, 2010.

WASHINGTON—U.S. Citizenship and Immigration Services (USCIS) announced nearly $8 million in grants for community-based organizations, unveiled a new Web-based Citizenship Resource Center, and discussed citizenship research and immigrant integration at a special Constitution Day and Citizenship Day conference.

The 2010 expanded citizenship and integration grant program and the new Web-based Citizenship Resource Center provide much-needed support for citizenship services in communities across America," said USCIS Director Alejandro Mayorkas. "By supporting the integration of those on the path to citizenship, we are able to send a welcoming message to those who aspire to become U.S. citizens, and at the same time proactively foster an increased understanding of the rights and responsibilities of U.S. citizenship that are so foundational to our experience as Americans."

Seventy-five organizations from 27 states and the District of Columbia will receive a total of $7.8 million in federal grant funding to promote citizenship education and immigrant integration in communities across the country.[145]

WHISTLEBLOWER ALERT—RETALIATION!

• **USCIS official's transfer probed: Whistle blown on 'negligence and mishandling' of records**—headline, *Washington Times,* October 19, 2010. "The Office of Special Counsel is investigating the involuntary transfer of a top official at U.S. Citizenship and Immigration Services who reported suspected "gross negligence and mishandling" of more than 600 certificates of citizenship and naturalization... Maria Aran, the immigration service's chief of staff in Miami, had been reassigned as a supervisory adjudications officer in Tampa, Fla., after reporting that hundreds of certificates of citizenship and naturalization had been voided without due cause, were unaccounted for, had not been verified as issued, were issued as duplicates, or were routinely left unsecured ... Ms. Aran had been given 10 days to accept the move or be terminated."[146]

Obama era: 2011

LAWLESSNESS ALERT!

Bypassing Congress the Obama administration creates more chaos, lawlessness (and backlogs) for immigration courts (courts are funded by tax dollars not legal immigrants and obviously not illegal aliens). On June 17, 2011, ICE Director John Morton issues a memorandum for all field officers to exercise prosecutorial discretion "consistent with the Civil Immigration Enforcement Priorities of the Agency for the Apprehensive, Detention and Removal of Aliens."[147] If you were an illegal alien who was denied, facing deportation or arrested, wouldn't you appeal?[148]

• **ICE agent's union speaks out on director's discretionary memo**—headline, *PR Newswire,* June 23, 2011.[149]

Union leaders around the nation issued a unanimous no confidence vote in ICE Director John Morton on behalf of ICE officers, *agents and employees nationwide citing gross mismanagement within the Agency as well as efforts within ICE to create backdoor amnesty through agency policy.* ICE Union leaders say that since the no confidence vote was released problems within the Agency have increased, citing the Director's latest Discretionary Memo as just one example.

"Any American concerned about immigration needs to brace themselves for what's coming," said Chris Crane, President of the National ICE Council which represents approximately 7,000 ICE agents, officers and employees, "this is just one of many new ICE policies in queue aimed at stopping the enforcement of U.S. immigration laws in the United States. Unable to pass its immigration agenda through legislation, the Administration is now implementing it through agency policy."

Crane emphasized that agents, officers, employees and the Union had no input in these policies, "ICE and the Administration have excluded our union and our agents from the entire process of developing policies, it was all kept secret from us, we found out from the newspapers. ICE worked hand-in-hand with immigrants' rights groups, but excluded its own officers."

Agents say the policy is a "law enforcement nightmare" developed by the Administration to win votes at the expense of sound and responsible law enforcement policy. "The desires of foreign nationals illegally in the United States were the framework from which these policies were developed," Crane said, "the result is a means for every person here illegally to avoid arrest or detention, as officers we will never know who we can or cannot arrest."

GET OUT THE VOTE ALERT!

Your tax dollars at work.

• **USCIS announces FY 2011 grant recipients during constitution week**—headline, *USCIS Press Release,* Sept. 21, 2011. "WASHINGTON-U.S. Citizenship and Immigration Services (USCIS) today announced the award of $9 million in grants to expand citizenship preparation programs for permanent residents. Forty-two organizations from 27 states and the District of Columbia will receive funding. The agency's Citizenship and Integration Grant Program has assisted more than 19,000 permanent residents since its launch in October 2009.[150] "This important announcement embodies USCIS's ongoing commitment to promote civic integration and citizenship among eligible permanent residents," said USCIS Director Alejandro Mayorkas. "Recognizing the demand for high-quality citizenship preparation programs, this funding will provide greatly needed services to approximately 20,000 permanent residents striving to become U.S. citizens."[151]

Be sure and visit the WelcomeUSA.gov website. [152]

LAWLESSNESS & ANTI-LEGAL IMMIGRATION ALERT!

It is still Vegas-like and awful at the USCIS if you are a legal immigrant and an American business owner. Poorly trained USCIS adjudicators issue random, lawless, arbitrary decisions against legal immigration. In the "culture of no," how many hard-working, honest legal immigrants did the USCIS deny and kick out is anybody's guess. It is especially tough for legal immigrants with extraordinary skills. Meanwhile politicians want to give citizenship to millions of illegal aliens telling the world that legal immigration and following the law in America is for suckers.[153].

• Panel discussion moderated by Frederick Troncone of the Ombudsman's Office—DHS, 2011. "This roundtable shared differing perspectives on recent USCIS employment-based adjudications, focusing primarily on predictability and consistency.

Panelists focused on the need for USCIS to better understand current business practices. Employer relocation trends demonstrate how companies strive to fulfill business objectives and enhance career development with international assignments. Companies are now utilizing more employee transfers than ever. Ms. Shotwell explained that based upon increased issuance of Requests for Evidence (RFEs), there is a perception that the government may be struggling to keep up with current business practices. All panelists agreed that USCIS needs to better understand the business community, such as the use of "virtual offices," and ensure better consistency. Ms. Nice stated that companies are increasingly under pressure and fast-paced. As companies must pivot to account for change, they may chose leave the United States and go elsewhere due to the complexity of the immigration process.

Panelists expressed concerns with the lack of predictability in USCIS employment-based processing. They reported that attorneys and their clients often receive varying results for similar petitions or applications. For example, H1-B specialty occupation petitions submitted for the same project have yielded different RFE's. Ms. Rahall stated that USCIS appears to be more restrictive now than in years past. She explained that inconsistency gives the appearance of a "culture of no" surrounding USCIS employment-based adjudications. Ultimately, companies may turn elsewhere to conduct business, and the United States may lose out.

Panelists commented that accountability for business-related immigration is limited because the USCIS appeals process is not timely enough for companies. Ms. Rahal shared that employers will often re-file petitions, rather than submitting an appeal due to the lengthy processing times."

UH-OH! USCIS MODERNIZATION PROGRAM ALERT!

• **Source: Government and Accountability Office Report:** Immigration Benefits: Consistent Adherence to DHS's Acquisition Policy Could Help Improve Transformation Program Outcomes, Nov 22, 2011, summary below. As of this writing, this is the most recent report on this topic. Recommendations outstanding.[154]

Each year, the Department of Homeland Security's (DHS) U.S. Citizenship and Immigration Services (USCIS) processes millions of applications for immigration benefits using a paper-based process. In 2005, USCIS embarked on a major, multiyear program to transform its process to a system that is to incorporate electronic application filing, adjudication, and case management. In 2007, GAO reported that USCIS was in the early stages of the Transformation Program and that USCIS's plans partially or fully met key practices. In 2008, USCIS contracted with a solutions architect to help develop the new system. As requested, GAO evaluated the extent to which USCIS has followed DHS acquisition policy in developing and managing the Transformation Program. GAO reviewed DHS acquisition management policies and guidance; analyzed transformation program planning and implementation documents such as operational requirements; compared schedule and cost information with GAO best practice guidance; and interviewed USCIS officials.

USCIS has not consistently followed the acquisition management approach that DHS outlined in its management directives in developing and managing the Transformation Program. USCIS awarded a solutions architect contract in November 2008, in effect selecting an acquisition approach before completing documents required by DHS management directives. Specifically, DHS's acquisition policy requires that prior to selecting an acquisition approach, programs establish operational requirements, develop a program baseline against which to measure progress, and complete a plan that outlines the program's acquisition strategy. *However, USCIS did not complete an Operational Requirements Document until October 2009, which was to inform the Acquisition Program Baseline and the Acquisition Plan. Consequently, USCIS awarded a solutions architect contract to begin capability development activities prior to having a full understanding of the program's operational requirements and the resources needed to execute the program. GAO has previously reported that firm requirements must be established and sufficient resources must be allocated at the beginning of an acquisition program, or the program's execution will be subpar. The lack of defined requirements, acquisition strategy, and associated cost parameters contributed to program deployment delays of over 2 years. In addition, through fiscal year 2011, USCIS estimates it will have spent about $703 million, about $292 million more than the original program baseline estimate. USCIS expects to begin deployment of the first release of the Transformation Program in December 2011. However, USCIS is continuing to manage the program without specific acquisition management controls, such as reliable schedules, which detail work to be performed by both the government and its contractor over the expected life of the program. As a result, USCIS does not have reasonable assurance that it can meet its future milestones. USCIS has established schedules for the first release of the Transformation Program, but GAO's analysis shows that these schedules are not reliable as they do not meet best practices for schedule estimating. For example, program schedules did not identify all activities to be performed by the government and solutions architect. Moreover, as outlined by DHS acquisition management guidance, a life-cycle cost estimate is a required and critical element in* *the acquisition process. USCIS has developed and updated the $1.7 billion life-cycle cost estimate for the Transformation Program, but USCIS's individual schedules for the Transformation Program did not meet best practices for schedule estimating, raising questions about the credibility of the program's life-cycle cost estimates. Because some program costs such as labor, supervision, and facilities cost more if the program takes longer, reliable schedules can contribute to an understanding of the cost impact if the program does not finish on time. Collectively, and moving forward, not meeting best practices increases the risk of schedule slippages and related cost overruns, making meaningful measurement and oversight of program status and progress, and accountability for results, difficult to achieve. GAO recommends that USCIS ensure its program schedules and life-cycle cost estimates are developed in accordance with best practices guidance.* DHS concurred with GAO's recommendations and outlined the actions that USCIS is taking or has taken to address each recommendation [italics mine]."

Obama era: 2012

DUH ALERT!

Some politicians have it wrong when they say illegal aliens are self–deporting because of the economy. That may be true but LEGAL immigrants are also leaving.

• **America Failing to Attract Immigrant Workers, Entrepreneurs: Report**—headline, *International Business Times,* May 24, 2012. "A scathing new report details the way the United States is failing to attract and retain the immigrant workers -- skilled and unskilled -- who are crucial to thriving in a global economy ... The conclusion: the United States is falling behind because of its "irrational and undirected" immigration policies."[155]

DEFACTO AMNESTY ALERT!

Creating more chaos and lawlessness at the immigration courts funded by taxpayers, DHS Chief Janet Napolitano issues a memo "Exercising Prosecutorial Discretion with Respect to Individuals Who Came to the United States as Children," to David V. Aguilar, Acting Commissioner, U.S. Customs and Border Protection,

Alejandro Mayorkas Director, USCIS, and John Morton Director, ICE. Meanwhile, where is the "prosecutorial discretion" for legal immigrants?

- **Exercising Prosecutorial Discretion with Respect to Individuals Who Came to the United States as Children**—*DHS Memo,* Janet Napolitano.[156]

By this memorandum, I am setting forth how, in the exercise of our prosecutorial discretion, the Department of Homeland Security (DHS) should enforce the Nation's immigration laws against certain young people who were brought to this country as children and know only this country as home. As a general matter, these individuals lacked the intent to violate the law and our ongoing review of pending removal cases is already offering administrative closure to many of them. However, additional measures are necessary to ensure that our enforcement resources are not expended on these low priority cases but are instead appropriately focused on people who meet our enforcement priorities. The following criteria should be satisfied before an individual is considered for an exercise of prosecutorial discretion pursuant to this memorandum:

- came to the United States under the age of sixteen;
- has continuously resided in the United States for a least five years preceding the date of this memorandum and is present in the United States on the date of this memorandum;
- is currently in school, has graduated from high school, has obtained a general education development certificate, or is an honorably discharged veteran of the Coast Guard or Armed Forces ofthe United States;
- has not been convicted of a felony offense, a significant misdemeanor offense, multiple misdemeanor offenses, or otherwise poses a threat to national security or public safety; and
- is not above the age of thirty.

PLAYING POLITICS ALERT!

More troubles for the USCIS and legal immigrants. Backlogs just got even bigger. Under Obama's latest defacto amnesty executive order, what will the 800,000 illegal aliens pay to have their work permits processed by the USCIS? Will they need background checks (I-485) like legal immigrants need? Will they be processed first or twenty-four years from now? It wouldn't be "fair" if they cut in the legal immigrant line, right?

• **Obama administration to stop deporting some young illegal immigrants**—headline, *CNN,* June 16, 2012. "In an election-year policy change, the Obama administration said Friday it will stop deporting young illegal immigrants who entered the United States as children if they meet certain requirements ... In a Rose Garden address Friday afternoon, President Barack Obama said the changes caused by his executive order will make immigration policy "more fair, more efficient and more just."'[157]

MIND-BENDING INCOMPETENCE ALERT!

• **U.S. citizen sues federal government after being wrongly flagged as deportable immigrant under Secure Communities program**—headline, *NBC News,* July 11, 2012. "A 25-year old Illinois man who says he was wrongly held in a maximum-security prison for two months after being incorrectly flagged by a controversial fingerprint-sharing system as a deportable immigrant is suing the federal government. James Aziz Makowski, who was born in India but has been a U.S. citizen since he was 1 year old, says he wound up in prison instead of boot camp as punishment for a drug crime, all due to errors in the government's fingerprint data-sharing system."[158]

LEGAL "PROFESSIONAL" IMMIGRANTS ARE BEING KICKED OUT ALERT!

As legal immigrants sit in limbo in backlogs the USCIS can send out RFE's (request for more evidence) to their American sponsors.

This happens *after* the legal immigrant has already been approved for a labor certification. Legal immigrants can *become illegal aliens* if the USCIS denies them via the RFEs. (RFEs are a recent invention). Indeed circumstances change during the lengthy wait times such as: Is the company still in business? Is the immigrant or employer still alive?

If legal immigrants cannot get processed swiftly (and that means "approved" or "denied" as to whether or not the immigrant can stay legally in America or must leave), is it still a mystery why America has an illegal alien/undocumented worker problem? This is *the real issue* that upsets and frustrates business leaders and corporate titans like Bill Gates. They are losing highly-skilled, professional legal immigrants thanks to the USCIS and Washington's failed leadership.

• **USCIS issues 3,000 requests for further evidence**—headline, *Marianas Variety*, July 13, 2012. "Petitions have yet to be adjudicated pending submission of documents required by U.S. Citizenship and Immigration Services for I-129CW petitions. According to USCIS regional media manager Marie Therese Sebrechts, "These have been issued for a variety of reasons ... It is not possible to make a final decision on these petitions until the employer provides a response," she said."[159]

• **More Indian applications for U.S. visas are refused**—headline, *Workpermit.com*, October 22, 2012. "USCIS has made it much harder for applicants to get H-1B and L-1 visas since 2008 and this is disproportionately affecting Indian applicants. The National Foundation for American Policy (NFAP), a think tank based in Arlington, Virginia, says that its analysis of USCIS figures shows that the tougher line is affecting Indian applicants particularly hard and that the tougher line is damaging the U.S. economy."[160]

LAWLESSNESS ALERT!

Are you a legal immigrant with an extraordinary ability? Brace yourself because chances are you could end up in court when the USCIS denies you and tries to kick you out. This is but one example of arbitrary decisions made by the agency. Check the courts for plenty more. Arbitrary=lawlessness and highly-skilled legal immigrants are turned into illegal aliens. Still wondering why there is an illegal alien problem?

• **Source: Citizenship and Immigration Services Ombusdman Annual Report 2012,** June 25, 2012, excerpt p. 16.[161]

"The first preference category (Employment-based) includes individuals with extraordinary ability; and outstanding professors, and researchers. The second preference category includes individuals of exceptional ability in the sciences, the arts, or business. On March 4, 2010, the Ninth Circuit Court of Appeals issued a decision, Poghos Kazarian v. U.S. Citizenship and Immigration Services (Kazarian), reviewing USCIS' application of the regulations governing extraordinary ability petitions. On December 22, 2010, USCIS issued a policy memorandum based on the Kazarian holding entitled, "Evaluation of Evidence Submitted with Certain Form I-140 Petitions; Revisions to the Adjudicator's Field Manual (AFM) Chapter 22.2, AFM Update AD11-14."

This memo provides a new two-pronged test to determine eligibility for the extraordinary ability, outstanding professor or researcher, and exceptional ability categories. The test requires: 1) an evaluation of whether the petitioner provided the requisite evidence; and 2) a final merits determination. Stakeholders raised the following concerns: 1) the subjective nature of a final merits determination; and 2) consistency in the application of the new policy. *Stakeholders contended that the policy memorandum permitted Immigration Services Officers (ISOs) too much discretion in making the final merits determination, leading to arbitrary decisions by adjudicators.*"

LEGAL IMMIGRANTS CAN BE DEPORTED BECAUSE ... ALERT!

Note to legal immigrants: Always, always send everything to the USCIS by certified mail because the agency sometimes loses documents, destroys them or makes mistakes (even with their new, fancy modernization online system) and they will put YOU in deportation. Suddenly your entire life will be turned upside down and you are now an illegal alien even though you followed the laws and had an immigration lawyer.

• **Court case 10-55889 v. Napolitano. Currently pending as of this writing at the Ninth Circuit, United States Court of Appeals**. Declaration Steven J. Pollnow, Assistant Center Director of the Nebraska Service Center, DHS, USCIS. "After adjudication, most temporary benefit receipt files are retired to a special contractor-run storage facility, and *they are destroyed after a designated retention period ranging from 6 months to 6 years* ... On October 3, 2006, the filing was initially assigned receipt number LIN-0700253248 by the mailroom contractor during data entry ... However, that same day (October 3, 2006), the contractor voided the mailout of the receipt notice for LIN-07-002-53248, and instead updated LIN-06-262-53196 (the rejected check/fee I-140 receipt) in systems as having been received in the mailroom on October 2, 2006. It is likely that the rejected Form I-140 bore the original LIN-06-262-53196 receipt bar code, so when it was returned with the correct fee on October 2, 2006, the contractor decided to keep using the original bar code and CLAIMS data rather than creating the petition again under the LIN-07-002-53248 number. The email from a customer service or other division of the Department of Homeland Security *erroneously states* that the I-140 LIN-07-002-53248 is "pending," when a complete review of CLAIMS shows that the I-140 receipt was voided. While *it is unfortunate* that the publically available "case status online' system at uscis.gov also indicates that LIN-007-002-53248 is an I-140 visa petition ... [immigrant] is aware that her employer's I-140 was, in fact, approved under receipt LIN-06-262-53196 [italics mine]."[162]

ILLEGAL IMMIGRANTS GET FREE PASS ALERT!

• **300,000 undocumented immigrants have applied for deportation reprieve**---headline, *Fox News Latino,* November 20, 2012. "In the three months since the Obama administration implemented a program that gives a reprieve from deportation to certain undocumented immigrants, about 300,000 have applied, reports the Christian Science Monitor. Some 50,000, or 17 percent, have been approved, the newspaper said, citing the United States Citizenship and Immigration Services, or USCIS. Approval enables immigrants to obtain work permits. "I am elated that so many applications are coming in and now that the fear of Romney winning is out of the way," said Rep. Luis Gutierrez, Illinois Democrat, in a statement quoted by the newspaper. "I think a half-million applications by New Year's should be our goal."[163]

CRIME & CORRUPTION ALERT!

• **Charges vs. woman accused of stealing a client's USCIS filing fees dismissed** (because she faces charges elsewhere in a district court)—headline, *Saipan Tribune,* February 2, 2012. The OAG said Castro was expected to process applications and mail money orders to USCIS, but instead she endorsed the money order to herself. The OAG only stated that the amount stolen from the victim was more than $250 but less than $20000.[164]

• **Top ICE figure pleads guilty in brazen $600G scam**—headline, *Fox News,* May 1, 2012. In a brazen criminal scheme to defraud taxpayers, one of the highest-ranking officials in the U.S. Immigration and Customs Enforcement agency pleaded guilty Tuesday in federal court to helping embezzle $600,000 from the federal government. Over three years, James Woosley and at least five other ICE employees scammed the agency by fabricating expenses for trips that were never taken and for hotel, rental car and restaurant expenses that did not exist, according to court records.[165]

• **Three men indicted for bribing immigration officials**—headline, *USCIS Status,* September 6, 2012. "Three men, two from Atlanta and one from New York, appeared in federal court Thursday, September 6, 2012, on charges that they conspired to bribe a federal immigration official in return for assistance with their immigration status, following an investigation by U.S. Immigration and Customs Enforcement's (ICE) Office of Professional Responsibility OPR). A federal grand jury indicted Hakeem Omar, 30, Ibrahim Barrie, 31, and Samuel Bolay, 24, Aug. 21 for conspiracy and bribery, and OPR special agents arrested all three men Sept. 5. "These defendants are charged with attempting to circumvent the immigration process by offering bribes to a federal agent," said United States Attorney Sally Quillian Yates. "The integrity of our immigration process has important implications for the security of our communities, and this case shows that we will take efforts to subvert this process seriously." "The ICE Office of Professional Responsibility considers bribery of our employees an extremely serious offense, as these actions can potentially undermine the security of our nation. We swiftly investigate all bribery attempts and take appropriate enforcement action when warranted," said David P. D'Amato, special agent in charge of OPR for the Southeast Region. According to information presented in court: Beginning in September 2010, and continuing until at least July, Omar, Barrie and Bolay paid bribes to an OPR special agent who was working in an undercover capacity, in exchange for immigration and other benefits."[166]

• **Los Angeles employment agency owner charged with filing bogus work visa applications**—headline, *ICE News Release,* November 1, 2012. "The owner of a Los Angeles employment agency was indicted Thursday on immigration fraud charges for allegedly filing more than 100 bogus work visa petitions on behalf of aliens she falsely claimed had been recruited for positions with prominent hospitals and non-profit organizations ... "Visa fraud crimes involve the unwitting and the desperate," said U.S. Attorney Andre Birotte Jr. "Tabafunda allegedly took this exploitation to new heights, falsely claiming associations with some of America's most trust organizations, including internationally known cancer centers."[167]

GET OUT THE VOTE ALERT! Your tax dollars at work.

• **USCIS announces FY 2012 citizenship and integration grant programs recipients**—headline, *USCIS Press Release,* Sept. 21, 2012. "On Sept. 17, 2012, U.S. Citizenship and Immigration Services (USCIS) announced the award of approximately $5 million in grants designed to promote immigrant civic integration and prepare permanent residents for citizenship. Under this program, 31 immigrant-serving organizations from 21 states and the District of Columbia will receive federal funding to support citizenship preparation services for permanent residents through September 2014 ... This is the fourth year USCIS has awarded competitive grant funding to immigrant-serving organizations to support citizenship preparation efforts. During the first three years of the program, USCIS awarded a total of $18.3 million through 111 grants to immigrant-serving organizations. To date, these organizations have provided citizenship preparation services to approximately 38,000 permanent residents in 30 states and the District of Columbia. USCIS anticipates an additional 26,000 permanent residents will receive citizenship preparation services by September 2014."[168]

Obama era: 2013

NATIONAL SECURITY ALERT!

• **Upholding the value of our citizenship: National security Threats Should be Denaturalized**, *Center of Immigration Studies,* January 2013.[169]

"This paper examines the surprising number of naturalized citizens who have been charged and convicted of serious national security crimes — including terrorism, espionage, and theft of sensitive information and technology — in the last several years. It compares the relative ease with which aliens naturalize with the extreme difficulty in stripping them of citizenship, even when they prove to be national security threats who have gamed the system. It also discusses the fact that the federal government, and the Department of Homeland Security in particular, have no systematic method of examining such cases to establish a baseline of "lessons learned" to attempt to weed out future threats, nor make any significant effort to denaturalize individuals even after they have committed serious national security offenses of the type described. It recommends that if the government will not or cannot take better care to prevent the admission of individuals who are serious threats to our safety, then it must move more aggressively to reverse its mistakes and strip citizenship from those who commit national security crimes against our nation.

Key findings include:

• In the past decade, dozens of naturalized U.S. citizens have been arrested and charged with a variety of serious national security-related offenses involving terrorism, spying, and theft of sensitive information and technology.
• The federal government almost never revokes the citizenship of these naturalized citizens, even when it is clear that they concealed material facts regarding their extreme ideas or associations with terrorist groups or foreign intelligence organizations at the time they naturalized.
• There is no central government repository of information about naturalized citizens who engage in serious national-security offenses.

• The Department of Homeland Security (DHS) has no systematic method for collecting the information nor efforts in place to review such cases, either for the purpose of instituting denaturalization or in order to discern whether there are steps it can and should take to better vet applicants during the naturalization process.

• Administrative naturalization continues unabated with hundreds of thousands being granted citizenship each year (over 6.5 million in the last decade).

• The consequence of these actions is to place all Americans at greater risk, as shown by the kinds of crimes for which many naturalized citizens have already been arrested, charged, convicted, and sentenced."

VOTE-GRAB ALERT!

The "Gang of Eight," a bi-partisan group of U.S. senators, introduces a framework to supposedly fix immigration that includes a path to citizenship for 11 million illegal aliens but it is really a vote-grab and make the crisis worse. No need to pretend anymore. As long serving Senator John McCain (R-Ariz.) stated: "The electoral politics of the issue had changed and that his [Republican] party needs to adapt on immigration if it wants to lure Latino voters.' Nice, lure Latino voters. Let's be blunt here. The Gang of Eight has just discriminated against all legal immigrants from every country around the world including those from Mexico who followed the laws and waited for years. The Gang of Eight has slapped the faces of every American who expects their lawmakers to adhere to the rule of law—not break laws. Comprehensive immigration reform is not about honoring the Constitution or serving America's interest. Illegal=legal. Legal=illegal. This is about power. *Their power.* Do you wonder why the Republican Party is on life support? Can you tell the difference between the two parties anymore? Are we clear yet?

• **Chuck, Schumer, John McCain: Immigrations odd couple—**headline, *Politico,* January 28, 2013. "A few days after Republicans took an electoral beating from Hispanic voters, Sen. Lindsey Graham made a phone call to Sen. Chuck Schumer. The South Carolina Republican wanted to restart the stalled talks with Schumer on immigration from a couple years back. But this time, he noted, his closest Senate friend was ready to reengage in the emotionally charged issue: John McCain."[170]

The Gang of Eight: The Republican senators: Marco Rubio (R-FL.), Jeff Flake (R-AZ), John McCain (R-AZ), and Lindsey Graham (R-SC). The Democrat senators: Dick Durbin (D-IL.), Chuck Schumer (D-NY), Michael Bennet (D-CO) and Robert Menendez (D-NJ),.[171]

PRESIDENT OBAMA JOINS GANG OF EIGHT ALERT!

Why follow the law, uphold the constitution, and do something positive for legal immigration and America when President Obama can create a permanent power base by legalizing millions of illegals/new voters? Why do you think he voted against comprehensive immigration reform when President George W. Bush was in office? He is America's first-community-organizer-in-chief. No need to pretend anymore. President Obama joins the "Gang of Eight" and takes it one step further by insisting that a path to citizenship becomes the law before enforcement of America's borders.[172]

• **Obama on immigration: reform must include path to citizenship**—headline, *Politico,* January 30, 2013. "The immigration reform plan President Barack Obama outlined Tuesday sounds a lot like the new bipartisan proposal from the Senate — and on the broad points, it is. But the differences are in the details. And those details, with the liberal stamp Obama put on his approach here, could be the difference between a deal and another failed effort on an issue that Washington has struggled with for years."[173]

ILLEGAL ALIEN ALERT!

A deportation hearing is scheduled for President Obama's Kenyan illegal alien Uncle Onyango Obama for December. He was originally deported in 1992—except he never left (wink, wink). Uncle Obama never would have been caught had it not been for that pesky drunk driving arrest in 2011. Could Uncle Obama be holding out for his nephew's potential amnesty law? After all, as you now know, waiting for another amnesty might be faster than following the laws like legal immigrants have learned the hard way.

• **Obama uncle in Mass. Gets Dec. deportation hearing**— headline, *Associated Press*, January 30, 2013. "A federal immigration judge has scheduled a new deportation hearing granted last year to President Barack Obama's uncle in Massachusetts. Onyango (ohn-YAHN'-goh) Obama is the half brother of the president's late father ... The 68-year-old Obama was ordered deported in 1992 after he failed to renew an application to stay."[174]

Had enough?

Obviously there are more government reports, and examples of crime and incompetence at America's immigration agency, I could include in this book. However, I think you get the picture now as to the reality of America's broken immigration system and what "legal immigration" actually has looked like for decades.

MARINKA PESCHMANN

14 •

WORKING AT DHS

Will the government (Democrats and Republicans) fix the immigration crisis they created or make it worse? Following is the oath America's lawmakers took when they were sworn into office.

"I do solemnly swear (or affirm) that I will support and defend the Constitution of the United States against all enemies, foreign and domestic; that I will bear true faith and allegiance to the same; that I take this obligation freely, without any mental reservation or purpose of evasion; and that I will well and faithfully discharge the duties of the office on which I am about to enter: So help me God."

I don't know what it is like for the USCIS employees who work within America's Vegas-like broken system. How do they, week after week, month after month, year after year, cash in their paychecks knowing full well how the system is broken, riddled with mind-bending incompetence and crime? How do they keep accepting new applications and cash legal immigrants' checks when they know that these new *legal* immigrants may not be processed for years, decades, if ever? What is it like for them to watch their colleagues indicted, year after year? Let's face it; taking bribes (seen as tips) is easy money. Who is going to tell?

I have never met a happy USCIS employee, but I have met some who have left the agency because they could not take working there any longer.

They could not take a system where often their hands were tied and they became nothing more than paper pushers, day in, depressing day out.[175] What kind of person can watch legal immigrants suffer in despair while dangling their freedom in their faces?

According to the *Government Accountability Office report: Taking Further Action to Better Determine Causes of Morale Problems Would Assist in*

Targeting Action Plans, released in September 2012, the answer includes low morale:[176]

"Department of Homeland Security (DHS) employees reported having lower average morale than the average for the rest of the federal government, but morale varied across components and employee groups within the department." According to the report, Immigration and Customs Enforcement (ICE) and Transportation Security Agency (TSA) employees suffer from the lowest morale. USCIS personnel felt there "was a lack of mission understanding on the part of their managers."

Indeed, America was a nation built by immigrants: an experiment on self–determination governance that became the shining beacon of hope, righteousness and opportunity for people around the world.

One cannot help but wonder if that will be true again.

APPENDIX

Original letter in Chapter 7: USCIS ATTACKS.

Please see my detailed response and interview request to Mr. Aytes at p. 68.

U.S. Department of Homeland Security
20 Massachusetts Avenue
Washington, D.C. 20529

**U.S. Citizenship
and Immigration
Services**

January 26, 2009

Editor
Canada Free Press
www.canadafreepress.com

Editor:

U. S. Citizenship and Immigration Services (USCIS) employees are some of the most experienced and highly skilled members of America's federal workforce. As the gatekeepers of the United States' immigration system, we all serve on the front lines of our homeland defense. And we, as any other organization with thousands of employees, are a reflection of our society and are not immune from instances when a few choose to abuse the authority entrusted in them. Your readers have a right to know -- and you have a responsibility to report -- how our agency deals with those few.

Unfortunately, your online paper chose to run an article on January 21 filled with errors and unsubstantiated information. Worse, it basically labeled this superb organization as one inhabited by 'crooks and thugs.' As an Immigration Officer with more than 30 years experience at both the former Immigration and Naturalization Service and USCIS, I simply cannot allow this story to stand.

Ensuring the integrity of the U.S. immigration system is our highest priority. When an individual fails to meet our high standards we work hard to ensure that justice is done, with appropriate and full punishment. That's the record. To further this important mission, USCIS established the Office of Security and Integrity (OSI) in 2007. In doing so, we tripled the resources dedicated to this critical mission and placed it under our executive leadership.

Through OSI's efforts, USCIS is well positioned to evaluate vulnerabilities, expose instances of corruption and create agency controls that minimize the effect a corrupt individual can have on our agency. OSI has also expanded its Investigations Division to receive complaints of alleged employee misconduct, corruption and fraud. We have in place an aggressive program that ensures employees know they are responsible for ensuring our agency's integrity.

Further, the article's accusation that "USCIS is overwhelmed by backlogs from immigrants following America's laws stuck in the nonsensical and degrading bureaucracy," ignores the fact that USCIS received nearly five million applications and petitions for immigrant benefits last year, yet we completed more than six and a half million cases. This substantially reduced processing times -- especially for naturalization.

I don't expect someone with very limited knowledge of the U.S. immigration system to be able to offer substantive or constructive criticism of agency policy and procedure. However, I do expect a reporter to stick

www.uscis.gov

Canada Free Press
Page 2

to the facts and refrain from offering editorial opinion in their work. This article served no other functional purpose other than to tarnish the honorable reputation of our employees and associate the entire USCIS workforce with criminals. It was shameful reporting and a deliberate smear that should not be counted as news.

At USCIS, we can't afford to make mistakes in our work. I challenge your paper to live up to these same high standards and seek to correct the inaccuracies of your story.

Sincerely,

Michael Aytes
Acting Deputy Director
U.S. Citizenship and Immigration Services

ABOUT THE AUTHOR

MARINKA PESCHMANN is a ghostwriter, journalist, writer and author. She has collaborated, ghostwritten, and contributed to books, film treatments, and stories from showbiz and celebrities to true crime, education, U.S. politics and the United Nations.

Having freelanced in the mainstream press and new media, Marinka no longer covers U.S. politics. She escaped media echo-chambers, having reported on problems crossing both sides of the political aisle.

When a journalist has been attacked by both sides, their work is done, given there are problems on both sides of the aisle.

How many times can one person write essentially the same story, over, and over again, where the names change?

Immigration remains broken.

ENDNOTES

Introduction

[1] Cindy Y. Rodriguez, "Latino vote key to Obama's re-election," *CNN,* November 9, 2012. Access online: http://www.cnn.com/2012/11/09/politics/latino-vote-key-election/index.html

[2] Ruby Cramer, "Obama Tells Hispanic Caucus Immigration Is "My Top Legislative Priority," *Buzzfeed.com,* January 25, 2013. http://www.buzzfeed.com/rubycramer/obama-tells-hispanic-caucus-immigration-is-my-top

[3] Julia Preston, "Obama Will Seek Citizenship Path in One Fast Push," *New York Times,* January 12, 2013.

[4] Brian Bennett, "Republicans senators present DREAM Act alternative," *Los Angeles Times,* November 27, 2012. Access online: http://articles.latimes.com/2012/nov/27/news/la-pn-republican-senators-dream-act-20121127

[5] Christina Wilkie, "John McCain on immigration reform: Path to citizenship, Dream Act must be included, *Huffingtonpost.com,* January 27, 2013. Access online: http://www.huffingtonpost.com/2013/01/27/john-mccain-immigration-reform_n_2561614.html

[6] Different versions of the *Dream Act,* the age for "children" begins at 12, 14 or 16. See Thomas.gov. or http://en.wikipedia.org/wiki/DREAM_Act

[7] *Government and Accountability Office Report: Immigration Benefits: Consistent Adherence to DHS's Acquisition Policy Could Help Improve Transformation Program Outcomes,* Nov 22, 2011, access online: http://www.gao.gov/products/GAO-12-66

[8] "Marco Rubio: Immigration Reform, Latino Voter Outreach Not Just Republican Problems," *Huffington Post,* August 29, 2012. Access online at: http://www.huffingtonpost.com/2012/08/29/marco-rubio-immigration_n_1838900.html Also see: Sunlen Miller, "McCain Tweets Support for Push on Immigration Reform," *ABC News,* November 9, 2012. Access online at: http://abcnews.go.com/blogs/politics/2012/11/mccain-tweets-support-for-push-on-immigration-reform/

Chapter 1: Legal in America? Not so Fast

[9] *State Department:* Diversity Visa Program: DV-2014 Entry Instructions: http://travel.state.gov/visa/immigrants/types/types_1318.html

[10] U.S. Labor Department on Prevailing Wages:
http://www.foreignlaborcert.doleta.gov/pwscreens.cfm
[11] National Guidelines http://www.foreignlaborcert.doleta.gov/pwscreens.cfm
http://www.doleta.gov/oa/bul10/Bulletin%202010-11a_Guideline_stnd_ij.pdf
[12] *State Department Visa bulletin:*
http://www.travel.state.gov/visa/bulletin/bulletin_5733.html
[13] USCIS:
http://www.uscis.gov/portal/site/uscis/menuitem.eb1d4c2a3e5b9ac89243c6a754
3f6d1a/?vgnextoid=816a83453d4a3210VgnVCM100000b92ca60aRCRD&vgnextc
hannel=816a83453d4a3210VgnVCM100000b92ca60aRCRD
[14] *State Department Visa Bulletin:*
http://www.travel.state.gov/visa/bulletin/bulletin_5803.html
[15] *State Department Visa Bulletin:*
http://www.travel.state.gov/visa/bulletin/bulletin_5803.html
[16] *State Department:* http://travel.state.gov/visa/immigrants/types/types_1306.htm
[17] "Obama on immigration: reform must include path to citizenship," *Politico,*
January 30, 2013. http://www.politico.com/story/2013/01/obama-immigration-
reform-citizenship-86879.html#ixzz2JeWtPt3C
[18] "Marco Rubio: Immigration Reform, Latino Voter Outreach Not Just
Republican Problems," *Huffington Post,* August 29, 2012. Access online at:
http://www.huffingtonpost.com/2012/08/29/marco-rubio-
immigration_n_1838900.html Also see: Sunlen Miller, "McCain Tweets Support
for Push on Immigration Reform," *ABC News,* November 9, 2012. Access online
at: http://abcnews.go.com/blogs/politics/2012/11/mccain-tweets-support-for-
push-on-immigration-reform/
[19] *Capital Immigration Law Group* PLLC:
http://www.cilawgroup.com/news/2008/07/21/receipt-numbers-explained-lin-
src-eac-wac/

Chapter 2: Take in Walk in the Shoes of Some Legal Immigrants

[20] "Legal immigrants: What about us?" *CNN,* February 1, 2013.
http://www.cnn.com/2013/02/01/us/legal-immigration-irpt
[21] *New York Times:* http://news.blogs.nytimes.com/2008/04/11/share-your-
immigration-story/?scp=3&sq=immigration%20blog%20stories&st=cse

Broken Immigration Timeline:

Chapter 3: President Ronald Reagan Era

[22] Access *GAO Report:* http://www.gao.gov/products/GGD-86-104BR
[23] *President Ronald Reagan's Remarks.* Access online:
http://www.reagan.utexas.edu/archives/speeches/1986/110686a.htm and here:
http://www.reagan.utexas.edu/archives/speeches/1986/110686b.htm

Immigration Reform and Control Act of 1986 bill text. Available here: https://secure.ssa.gov/apps10/poms.nsf/lnx/0500501440!opendocument
[24] Available here: http://www.nytimes.com/1987/04/06/us/us-is-expanding-amnesty-program-for-illegal-aliens.html
[25] *GAO Report*: http://www.gao.gov/products/NSIAD-88-92BR
[26] "Chuck, Schumer, John McCain: Immigrations odd couple," *Politico*, January 28, 2013. http://www.politico.com/story/2013/01/immigration-reform-deal-senate-schumer-mccain-86840.html#ixzz2JMHS7wMx

Chapter 4: President George H.W. Bush Era

[27] *GAO Report*: http://www.gao.gov/products/T-GGD-91-48
[28] *Philadelphia Inquirer:* http://articles.philly.com/1992-07-01/news/26029287_1_illegal-aliens-sting-operation-bribes

Chapter 5: President Bill Clinton era

[29] *GAO Report:* http://www.gao.gov/products/T-GGD-93-18
[30] *GAO Report:* http://www.gao.gov/products/T-GGD-93-39
[31] *Washington Post*: http://www.washingtonpost.com/wp-srv/politics/govt/admin/stories/reno021293.htm
[32] *New York Daily News*: http://www.nydailynews.com/news/politics/homeland-chief-michael-chertoff-home-cleaned-illegal-immigrants-article-1.358533#ixzz2JbPnpzvP
[33] *New York Times*: http://www.nytimes.com/1994/09/12/us/in-immigration-labyrinth-corruption-comes-easily.html
[34] *New York Times*: http://www.nytimes.com/1994/09/12/us/one-broker-s-slide-into-bribery.html
[35] David Schippers, Chief Investigative Counsel for the Clinton Impeachment's *Sell Out: The Inside Story of President Clinton's Impeachment* (Regnery Publishing, Inc. 2000). See: Chapter 4: Injustice for all.
[36] *Vanity Fair*: http://www.vanityfair.com/fame/features/2001/01/rocancourt200101
[37] *NBC Dateline special*: http://www.youtube.com/watch?v=UOKjR2yIc9Q&feature=relmfu
[38] *New York Times* article: http://www.nytimes.com/1998/03/13/nyregion/7-ins-employees-and-26-others-are-charged-with-selling-false-immigration-papers.html?scp=1&sq=continues%20to%20raise%20questions%20about%20how%20well%20the%20agency%20is%20addressing%20its%20vulnerability%20to%20corruption.%20The%20scheme%20grew%20so%20brazen,%20prosecutors%20said,%20that%20some%20cash%20bribes%20were%20exchanged%20right%20inside%20the%20INS%20offices%20at%2026%20Federal%20Plaza%20in%20downtown%20Manhattan&st=cse
[39] *VisaLaw.com*: http://www.visalaw.com/98sep/12sep98.html

[40] USCIS: http://www.uscis.gov/ilink/docView/FR/HTML/FR/0-0-0-1/0-0-0-42380/0-0-0-51326/0-0-0-51360.html

[41] *Associated Press*: http://amarillo.com/stories/062099/new_LG3039.001.shtml

[42] *GAO Report:* http://www.gao.gov/products/GGD-00-185

[43] *USCIS 'alien':*
http://www.uscis.gov/portal/site/uscis/menuitem.5af9bb95919f35e66f614176543f6d1a/?vgnextoid=d8571a5ec88d1310VgnVCM100000082ca60aRCRD&vgnextchannel=6d42dd1d5fd37210VgnVCM100000082ca60aRCRD

[44] *DHS 'alien':* http://www.dhs.gov/directing-requests-proper-components

Chapter 6: President George W. Bush Era

[45] *GAO Report:* http://www.gao.gov/products/GAO-01-488

[46] *GAO Report:* http://www.gao.gov/products/GAO-02-66

[47] *CNN:* http://archives.cnn.com/2002/US/03/12/inv.flight.school.visas/

[48] *CNN:* http://archives.cnn.com/2002/US/03/21/ins.woes/index.html

[49] *Eduardo Aguirre Jr., entire statement:*
http://www.uscis.gov/files/testimony/CIS_Budget_03_30_04.pdf

[50] *Washington Post:* http://www.washingtonpost.com/wp-dyn/content/article/2008/11/06/AR2008110602068_pf.html

[51] *Washington Times:*
http://www.washingtontimes.com/news/2004/dec/6/20041206-102115-6766r/?page=all

[52] *ImmigrationVoice:* Backlog elimination Centers opened in 2004 and closed in 2007.
http://immigrationvoice.org/wiki/index.php/Backlog_Center

[53] *GAO Report:* http://www.gao.gov/products/GAO-04-309R

[54] *Senate Hearing Transcript:*
http://commdocs.house.gov/committees/judiciary/hju94287.000/hju94287_0f.htm

[55] *GAO Report:* http://www.gao.gov/products/GAO-05-526

[56] *CIS Report:* http://www.cis.org/articles/2005/kephart.html

[57] *Washington Post:* http://www.washingtonpost.com/wp-dyn/content/article/2006/11/28/AR2006112801402.html

[58] *GAO Report:* http://www.gao.gov/products/GAO-06-895T

[59] *Associated Press:* http://www.usatoday.com/news/nation/2006-09-24-border-cases_x.htm

[60] *Associated Press:* http://usatoday30.usatoday.com/news/nation/2006-09-24-border-cases_x.htm

[61] *Washington Post:* http://www.washingtonpost.com/wp-dyn/content/article/2006/11/30/AR2006113000603.html

[62] *President George Bush Executive Order 13404:* http://www.gpo.gov/fdsys/pkg/FR-2006-06-12/pdf/06-5351.pdf

[63] *Bush's Executive Order 13404:* http://www.gpo.gov/fdsys/pkg/FR-2006-06-12/pdf/06-5351.pdf

[64] *Newsmax:*
http://archive.newsmax.com/archives/articles/2006/6/13/154454.shtml

[65] *GAO Report*: http://www.gao.gov/products/GAO-09-180
[66] "President Obama vs. Senator Obama on immigration," *Washington Post*: http://www.washingtonpost.com/blogs/wonkblog/wp/2012/06/24/president-obama-vs-senator-obama-on-immigration/
[67] 46-53, immigration bill goes down in defeat, *The Hill,* June 28, 2007. http://thehill.com/homenews/news/12430-46-53-immigration-bill-goes-down-in-defeat
[68] *Washington Times*: http://www.washingtontimes.com/news/2007/aug/15/us-agents-accused-of32aiding-islamist-scheme/
[69] *Indictment:* ." http://ca10.washburnlaw.edu/cases/2007/06/06-1296.htm
[70] *Citizenship Promotion Act 2007*: http://www.govtrack.us/congress/bills/110/s795
[71] *GAO Report:* http://www.gao.gov/assets/600/591649.pdf
[72] *Lofgren* press release: http://www.lofgren.house.gov/
[73] *Washington Post*: http://www.washingtonpost.com/wp-dyn/content/article/2008/11/06/AR2008110602068_pf.html
[74] *New York Times*: http://www.nytimes.com/2008/03/21/nyregion/21immigrant.html?ex=1363838400&en=68dec5bf354dcb45&ei=5124&partner=permalink&exprod=permalink
[75] *Indictment:* http://www.justice.gov/usao/gan/press/2008/05-14-08.pdf
[76] *Associated Press:* http://www.huffingtonpost.com/2008/12/05/top-homeland-security-off_n_148896.html
[77] *GAO Report*: http://www.gao.gov/products/GAO-08-940

Chapter 7: USCIS Attacks

[78] Original article *Peschmann archives*
[79] *Michael Aytes bio*: http://www.uscis.gov/portal/site/uscis/menuitem.5af9bb95919f35e66f614176543f6d1a/?vgnextoid=e4281e7617a7e010VgnVCM1000000ecd190aRCRD&vgnextchannel=c0fbab0a43b5d010VgnVCM10000048f3d6a1RCRD
[80] *Marinka Peschmann*, "Crime and Corruption at the U.S. Citizenship & Immigration Services," *CFP Archives*, January 21, 2009. http://www.marinkapeschmann.com/2009/01/21/crime-and-corruption-at-the-us-citizenship-immigration-services/
Also see: Michael Aytes bio, *USCIS website*. http://www.uscis.gov/portal/site/uscis/menuitem.5af9bb95919f35e66f614176543f6d1a/?vgnextoid=e4281e7617a7e010VgnVCM1000000ecd190aRCRD&vgnextchannel=c0fbab0a43b5d010VgnVCM10000048f3d6a1RCRD
[81] Access online: http://www.washingtontimes.com/news/2007/aug/15/us-agents-accused-of32aiding-islamist-scheme/
[82] *Indictment/ Press Release*: http://www.justice.gov/usao/gan/press/2008/05-14-08.pdf
[83] *Court records*: http://ca10.washburnlaw.edu/cases/2007/06/06-1296.htm
[84] Nina, Bernstein, "An Agent, A Green Card, and a Demand for Sex," *New York Times,* March 21, 2008.

http://www.nytimes.com/2008/03/21/nyregion/21immigrant.html?_r=4&oref=s login&ref=us&pagewanted=print&
[85] Julia Preston, "Readers Share Immigration Stories," *New York Times,* April 11, 2008. http://news.blogs.nytimes.com/2008/04/11/share-your-immigration-story/?scp=3&sq=immigration%20blog%20stories&st=cse

Chapter 8: Terrorists Have Applied for Green Cards

[86] *Peschmann archives:* http://www.marinkapeschmann.com/2010/03/15/immigration-reform-terrorists-have-applied-for-green-cards/
[87] *GAO Report:* http://www.gao.gov/products/GAO-09-55
[88] *GAO Report:* http://www.gao.gov/products/GAO-09-55
[89] "Immigration's Gang of 8: Who are they?" *Washington Post,* January 28, 2013. http://www.washingtonpost.com/blogs/the-fix/wp/2013/01/28/immigrations-gang-of-8-who-are-they/
[90] *Washington Post:* http://www.washingtonpost.com/wp-dyn/content/article/2008/11/06/AR2008110602068_pf.html

Chapter 9: Legal Immigration Bailout

[91] Washington Post: http://www.washingtonpost.com/wp-dyn/content/article/2008/11/06/AR2008110602068.html
[92] JW Exposes Illegal Alien Cop Killer's Extensive Criminal History, *Judicial Watch,* July 20, 2011. http://www.judicialwatch.org/blog/2011/07/jw-exposes-illegal-alien-cop-killer-s-extensive-criminal-history/
[93] *Peschmann archives:* http://www.marinkapeschmann.com/2009/01/15/the-immigration-bailout/]

Chapter 10: Game Changer

[94] Original article at *marinkapeschmann*.com archives.
[95] Citizenship USA (CUSA): Where Hillary's Latino votes came from, *Michelle Malkin.com,* February 6, 2008. http://michellemalkin.com/2008/02/06/where-hillarys-latino-votes-came-from/
[96] *Citizenship and Integration Grant Program:* http://www.uscis.gov/portal/site/uscis/menuitem.eb1d4c2a3e5b9ac89243c6a754 3f6d1a/?vgnextoid=ea0e0b89284a3210VgnVCM100000b92ca60aRCRD&vgnextc hannel=ea0e0b89284a3210VgnVCM100000b92ca60aRCRD
Citizenship Promotion Act of 2007: http://www.govtrack.us/congress/bills/110/s795
[97] *The Whistleblower: How the Clinton White House Stayed in Power to Reemerge in the Obama White House and on the World Stage* (One Rock Ink 2012). http://www.amazon.com/gp/product/0987834304/ref=as_li_qf_sp_asin_il?ie=U

TF8&tag=marinkapeschm-
20&linkCode=as2&camp=1789&creative=9325&creativeASIN=0987834304
[98] *Sell Out: The Inside Story of President Clinton's Impeachment,* (Regnery Publishing, Inc. 2000).
http://www.amazon.com/gp/product/0895261952/ref=as_li_qf_sp_asin_tl?ie=U
TF8&tag=marinkapeschm-
20&linkCode=as2&camp=217145&creative=399373&creativeASIN=0895261952
[99] *Homeland Security Act:* http://articles.cnn.com/2002-11-
25/politics/homeland.security_1_new-department-homeland-security-head-department?_s=PM:ALLPOLITICS
USCIS's Office of Citizenship (OoC):
http://www.uscis.gov/portal/site/uscis/menuitem.eb1d4c2a3e5b9ac89243c6a754
3f6d1a/?vgnextoid=a5e314c0cee47210VgnVCM100000082ca60aRCRD&vgnextch
annel=a5e314c0cee47210VgnVCM100000082ca60aRCRD
[100] *Executive Order 13404:* http://www.presidency.ucsb.edu/ws/index.php?pid=118
[101] *USCIS' Citizenship and Integration Grant Program:*
http://www.uscis.gov/portal/site/uscis/menuitem.749cabd81f5ffc8fba713d10526
e0aa0/?vgnextoid=19248e4f61e3a210VgnVCM100000b92ca60aRCRD&vgnextcha
nnel=2905df6bdd42a210VgnVCM100000b92ca60aRCRD
OoC:
http://www.uscis.gov/portal/site/uscis/menuitem.eb1d4c2a3e5b9ac89243c6a754
3f6d1a/?vgnextoid=a5e314c0cee47210VgnVCM100000082ca60aRCRD&vgnextch
annel=a5e314c0cee47210VgnVCM100000082ca60aRCRD
[102] *Cecilia Muñoz White House bio*:
http://www.whitehouse.gov/blog/author/Cecilia%20Mu%C3%B1oz
[103] *Immigrant Integration: U.S. Citizenship and Immigration Services Could Better Assess Its Grant Program,* GAO-12-274, Dec 16, 2011. http://www.gao.gov/products/GAO-12-274
[104] *Access California Services*: http://www.accesscal.org/
Central American Resource Center: http://www.carecendc.org/
International Rescue Committee, Inc. (IRC): http://www.rescue.org/board-and-overseers
[105] *Citizenship and Integration Grant Program:*
http://www.uscis.gov/portal/site/uscis/menuitem.eb1d4c2a3e5b9ac89243c6a754
3f6d1a/?vgnextoid=ea0e0b89284a3210VgnVCM100000b92ca60aRCRD&vgnextc
hannel=ea0e0b89284a3210VgnVCM100000b92ca60aRCRD
[106] *Citizenship and Integration Grant Program:*
http://www.uscis.gov/portal/site/uscis/menuitem.eb1d4c2a3e5b9ac89243c6a754
3f6d1a/?vgnextoid=ea0e0b89284a3210VgnVCM100000b92ca60aRCRD&vgnextc
hannel=ea0e0b89284a3210VgnVCM100000b92ca60aRCRD
[107] Cindy Y. Rodriguez, "Latino vote key to Obama's re-election," *CNN,* November 9, 2012. Access online:
http://www.cnn.com/2012/11/09/politics/latino-vote-key-election/index.html
[108] Facts on immigration in the United States, *CNN,* June 15, 2012.
http://news.blogs.cnn.com/2012/06/15/facts-on-immigration-in-the-united-states/

[109] Peschmann archives, September 30, 2012.
http://www.marinkapeschmann.com/2012/09/30/game-changer-how-president-bush-could-help-president-obama-win-re-election/

Chapter 11: President Barack Obama Era

[110] *DHS Directive*: http://www.cfpnewswatch.com/pdf-files/DHSbacklogs.pdf
[111] *Peschmann archives*: http://www.marinkapeschmann.com/2009/03/18/crime-corruption-and-incompetence-at-the-us-citizenship-immigration-services-part-ii/
[112] *GAO Report:* http://www.gao.gov/products/GAO-09-180
[113] *Court records*: http://www.marinkapeschmann.com/wp-content/uploads/2009/10/US_v_RoyBailey_usgsentmemo.pdf
[114] *City Journal:* http://www.city-journal.org/2009/19_4_corruption.html
[115] *Associated Press:* http://www.highbeam.com/doc/1A1-D96IT40O4.html, *U.S. State Department Press Release*: http://www.state.gov/m/ds/rls/126748.htm
[116] *Detroit News* via *Family Security Matters:*
http://www.familysecuritymatters.org/publications/id.2713/pub_detail.asp
[117] *New York Times:*
http://www.nytimes.com/2009/06/17/nyregion/17scheme.html?_r=1&pagewanted=all
[118] *New York Law Journal:*
http://www.law.com/jsp/article.jsp?id=1202432257655&slreturn=1
[119] *ABC News*: http://abcnews.go.com/Politics/corrupt-border-officials-accepting-bribes-illegal-immigrants-exposes/story?id=8654516
[120] *Peschmann archives*: http://www.marinkapeschmann.com/2009/02/04/us-citizenship-immigration-services-blasts-journalist-over-crime-corruption-story-journalist-fires-back/
[121] *2009 Virginia Threat Assessment*:
http://www.marinkapeschmann.com/2010/05/24/radical-islamic-terrorists-and-america%e2%80%99s-immigration-crisis/
[122] *Immigration attorney Carl Shusterman:*
http://blogs.ilw.com/carlshusterman/2009/04/eb3-category-to-close-down-on-may-1st.html

Chapter 13: President Obama Era, Part II

[123] *Associated Press:* http://www.usatoday.com/news/nation/2010-03-08-student-visa-fraud-ring_N.htm
[124] *Department of Justice* press release: http://www.fbi.gov/losangeles/press-releases/2010/la042010.htm
[125] *Nexgov:* http://www.nextgov.com/technology-news/2010/07/gao-sting-shows-passport-fraud-remains-a-problem/47272/
[126] *Fox News*: http://www.foxnews.com/us/2010/05/26/terror-alert-mexican-border/#ixzz1zlo12ZbM

[127] *Legal immigrant user fee schedule USCIS:*
http://www.uscis.gov/portal/site/uscis/menuitem.eb1d4c2a3e5b9ac89243c6a754
3f6d1a/?vgnextchannel=b1ae408b1c4b3210VgnVCM100000b92ca60aRCRD&vgn
extoid=b1ae408b1c4b3210VgnVCM100000b92ca60aRCRD
[128] *GAO Report:* http://www.gao.gov/products/GAO-10-560T
[129] N-400 Application for Naturalization, *DHS/USCIS*, part 10, p. 7.
http://www.uscis.gov/files/form/n-400.pdf
[130] *Bloomberg press release:*
http://www.nyc.gov/portal/site/nycgov/menuitem.c0935b9a57bb4ef3daf2f1c701
c789a0/index.jsp?pageID=mayor_press_release&catID=1194&doc_name=http%
3A%2F%2Fwww.nyc.gov%2Fhtml%2Fom%2Fhtml%2F2010a%2Fpr287-
10.html&cc=unused1978&rc=1194&ndi=1
[131] "Bloomberg plans big immigration Push," *Wall Street Journal*, June 23, 2010. *Fox*
interview video is embedded.
http://online.wsj.com/article/SB10001424052748703900004575325412638269010
.html
[132] *CIS Report:*
http://www.dhs.gov/xlibrary/assets/cisomb_annual_report_2009.pdf
[133] *New York Times:*
http://www.nytimes.com/2010/05/30/us/30visas.html?ref=us&_r=0

Chapter 12: Folly of the Politicians' Green Card for Investor Idea

[134] *Peschmann Archives:*
http://www.marinkapeschmann.com/2010/06/28/immigration-reform-mayor-
bloomberg%E2%80%99s-green-card-for-investors-idea-is-already-law/
[135] *Peschmann Archives:* http://www.marinkapeschmann.com/2010/09/27/video-
broken-immigration-mayor-michael-bloomberg-declines-to-discuss-his-solution-
that-is-already-law/
[136] *Citizenship and Immigration Services Ombudsman Annual Report to Congress 2010.*
http://www.dhs.gov/xlibrary/assets/cisomb_2010_annual_report_to_congress.pd
f
[137] *Peschmann archives:* http://www.marinkapeschmann.com/2010/09/27/video-
broken-immigration-mayor-michael-bloomberg-declines-to-discuss-his-solution-
that-is-already-law/
[138] *2012 CIS Ombudsman's Annual Report:*
http://www.dhs.gov/xlibrary/assets/cisomb-2012-annualreportexecsummary.pdf
Link to full report: http://www.dhs.gov/xlibrary/assets/cisomb-2012-
annualreport.pdf
[139] Access all *CIS Reports:*
http://www.dhs.gov/files/publications/gc_1301971419354.shtm
[140] *Huffingtonpost.com:* http://www.huffingtonpost.com/2012/06/11/record-
number-of-immigran_n_1587323.html
[141] *Associated Press:* http://www.pjstar.com/free/x551366486/18-immigrants-sue-
U-S-over-entry-program-denials

[142] *Press release*: http://www.prweb.com/releases/2012/10/prweb9982204.htm

[143] http://www.cbsnews.com/8301-503544_162-20005151-503544.html

[144] *USCIS Press Release*:
http://www.uscis.gov/portal/site/uscis/menuitem.5af9bb95919f35e66f614176543
f6d1a/?vgnextoid=ffb01c7dcb507210VgnVCM100000082ca60aRCRD&vgnextcha
nnel=a2dd6d26d17df110VgnVCM1000004718190aRCRD

[145] *USCIS Press Release*:
http://www.uscis.gov/portal/site/uscis/menuitem.5af9bb95919f35e66f614176543
f6d1a/?vgnextoid=0ef8ef6b56c1b210VgnVCM100000082ca60aRCRD&vgnextcha
nnel=a2dd6d26d17df110VgnVCM1000004718190aRCRD

[146] *Washington Times*: http://www.washingtontimes.com/news/2010/oct/19/uscis-
officials-transfer-probed/#ixzz2DT0yYkuk

[147] *Morton memo*: http://www.marinkapeschmann.com/2011/06/23/ice-agents-
obama-administration-using-agency-policy-for-backdoor-amnesty/

[148] *Morton Memo:* http://www.marinkapeschmann.com/2011/06/23/ice-agents-
obama-administration-using-agency-policy-for-backdoor-amnesty/

[149] *ICE Agents Press Release:* http://www.prnewswire.com/news-releases/ice-agents-
union-speaks-out-on-directors-discretionary-memo-124441368.html

[150] *Citizenship and Integration Grant Program*: http://www.uscis.gov/grants

[151] *USCIS Press Release:*
http://www.uscis.gov/portal/site/uscis/menuitem.5af9bb95919f35e66f614176543
f6d1a/?vgnextoid=2b9aa0920dc82310VgnVCM100000082ca60aRCRD&vgnextch
annel=a2dd6d26d17df110VgnVCM1000004718190aRCRD

[152] *Welcome toUSA.gov:* http://www.welcometousa.gov/

[153] *Panel discussion summary and transcript.* https://www.dhs.gov/importance-
adjudication-predictability-impact-employers-individuals-and-economy

[154] *GAO Report:* http://www.gao.gov/products/GAO-12-66

[155] *International Business Times:*
http://www.ibtimes.com/articles/344857/20120524/immigrant-labor-workers-
visas-h1b-visa-entrepreneurs.htm

[156] *DHS Memo:* http://www.dhs.gov/xlibrary/assets/s1-exercising-prosecutorial-
discretion-individuals-who-came-to-us-as-children.pdf

[157] *CNN:* http://www.cnn.com/2012/06/15/politics/immigration/index.html

[158] *NBC News:* http://usnews.nbcnews.com/_news/2012/07/11/12665799-us-
citizen-sues-federal-government-after-being-wrongly-flagged-as-deportable-
immigrant-under-secure-communities-program

[159] *Marianas Variety*: http://www.mvariety.com/cnmi/cnmi-news/local/47975-
uscis-issues-3000-requests-for-further-evidence.php

[160] *Workpermit.com*: http://www.workpermit.com/news/2012-10-22/more-indian-
applications-for-us-visas-are-Ukrefused

[161] *CIS Report 2012*: http://www.dhs.gov/xlibrary/assets/cisomb-2012-
annualreport.pdf

[162] *DHS/USCIS employee Steven J. Pollnow Declaration*:
http://marinkapeschmann/endnotes

[163] *Fox News Latino*:
http://latino.foxnews.com/latino/politics/2012/11/20/300000-undocumented-immigrants-have-applied-for-obama-administration/#ixzz2I6cT3Qlh
[164] *Sainpan Tribunes:*
http://www.saipantribune.com/newsstory.aspx?cat=1&newsID=116200
[165] *Fox News* article: http://www.foxnews.com/politics/2012/05/01/top-ice-figure-expected-to-plead-guilty-to-brazen-500g-scam/#ixzz1zhjeK2Ej
[166] *USICS Status*: http://uscisstatus.blogspot.ca/2012/09/three-men-indicted-for-bribing.html
[167] *Ice News Release*: http://www.aila.org/content/default.aspx?docid=41977
[168] *USCIS Press Release:*
http://www.uscis.gov/portal/site/uscis/menuitem.749cabd81f5ffc8fba713d10526e0aa0/?vgnextoid=1564df6bdd42a210VgnVCM100000b92ca60aRCRD&vgnextchannel=1564df6bdd42a210VgnVCM100000b92ca60aRCRD
[169] *Center for Immigration Studies Report:* http://cis.org/sites/default/files/reasoner-denatz.pdf
[170] *Politico:* http://www.politico.com/story/2013/01/immigration-reform-deal-senate-schumer-mccain-86840.html#ixzz2JOxEOczY
[171] "Immigration's Gang of 8: Who are they?" *Washington Post,* January 28, 2013. http://www.washingtonpost.com/blogs/the-fix/wp/2013/01/28/immigrations-gang-of-8-who-are-they/
[172] "Obama on immigration: reform must include path to citizenship," *Politico,* January 30, 2013. http://www.politico.com/story/2013/01/obama-immigration-reform-citizenship-86879.html#ixzz2JeWtPt3C
[173] *Politico:* http://www.politico.com/story/2013/01/obama-immigration-reform-citizenship-86879.html#ixzz2JeWtPt3C
[174] *Associated Press:* http://www.miamiherald.com/2013/01/30/3209013/obama-uncle-in-mass-gets-dec-deportation.html#storylink=cpy
[175] Also see: *Question and Answer Session with a former USCIS Adjudicator.* http://www.visajourney.com/content/adjudicator-q-and-a

Chapter 14: Working at DHS

[176] *GAO Morale Report:* http://www.gao.gov/assets/650/648997.pdf

www.ingramcontent.com/pod-product-compliance
Lightning Source LLC
Chambersburg PA
CBHW071132280326
41935CB00010B/1199

* 9 7 8 0 9 8 7 8 3 4 3 4 8 *